English is Crazy

*The spoken word and the written
— there is an astonishing gulf between them.*

HERCULE POIROT

Copyright © 2009, 2013, 2022 Judy Thompson

Also by Judy Thompson

English Phonetic Alphabet Workbook©
Companion to CHAPTER ONE of English is Crazy

How Do You Say?
Pronunciation and Expressions Sound Dictionary

Published in 2012 as *Grass is Black*

Speaking Made Simple
Speaking Course Curriculum©

(PDF Format only)

available from **thompsonlanguagecenter.com**

Backpacker's Guide to Teaching English
BOOK 1 **Cracking the Code** – on Pronunciation
BOOK 2 **Need For Speed** – on Conversation
BOOK 3 **You Don't Say** – on Fluency

ABC Facilitated Reading
An interactive literacy system for teaching reading at home

English is Crazy

Introducing the

English Phonetic Alphabet

by

Judy Thompson

All rights reserved.

This work is the intellectual property of the author. This book contains material protected under International and Federal Copyright Laws and Treaties. Any unauthorized reprint or use of this material is prohibited. No part of this publication may be reproduced, distributed, or transmitted in any form or by any means, including photocopying, recording, or other electronic or mechanical methods, without the prior written permission of the publisher, except in the case of brief quotations embodied in critical reviews and certain other noncommercial uses permitted by copyright law. For permission requests, email: **judy@thompsonlanguagecenter.com**

Thompson Language Center
Niagara, Ontario, Canada

www.ThompsonLanguageCenter.com
email: judy@thompsonlanguagecenter.com

Published by Thompson Language Center
Developed in Canada

Fourth Edition 2022
New title: **English is Crazy**
ISBN: **978-1-7781823-0-3**
Copyright © 2009, 2013 and 2022 by Judy Thompson
Copyright © 2001 original idea by Judy Thompson, English is Crazy is a registered trademark.
Third Edition 2013: English is Stupid – Students Are Not
(Original title) ISBN: 978-0-9812058-2-3

Special discounts are available on quantity purchases from Amazon.

NOTE: If you have received a copy of this document and have not paid for it, please remit $35.00 US to **judy@thompsonlanguagecenter.com** through PayPal or etransfer. Any unauthorized copying of this copyrighted book in either print or download version, will be subject to prosecution to the full extent of the law.

Every effort has been made to trace ownership of all copyrighted material and to secure permission from copyright holders. In the event of any question arising as to the use of any material, we would be pleased to make the necessary corrections in future printings.

Edited by: Marta Baziuk, Sandy Leppan and Noreen Brigden
Illustrated by: Suzanne Miller
Clipart by: Art Explosion Image Library CD-Rom Portfolio
Text design by: Noreen Brigden
Cover design by: Gillian Stead
Cover photography by Donna Brown

Printed in USA

To my students,
for everything they taught me.

Acknowledgements

Special thanks to my family: Ryan, Morgan, Brennan,
Ayden, Shayna, Erin, Julia, Collin, Shauna and Taiya.

Many thanks to my friends and co-workers
for their stand for me, these ideas, or both.

Gillian Stead, John Denison, Monica Long,
Noreen Brigden, Shannon Smith, Jennifer MacAulay,
Lydia Aeillo, Kathryn Brillinger, Ray Young,
Sandy Leppan and Carla Moray.

Also to Landmark Education,
for believing in me and my possibility.

Contents

PREFACE		9
INTRODUCTION		13
HOW THIS BOOK WORKS		24

PART ONE

BASIC

CHAPTER ONE — Spelling is Random 29

The Sounds of Letters

Ancient History, One Alphabet,
Book within a Book – **The English Phonetic Alphabet** 33–75
Silent Consonants, Vowel Sounds, Consonant Sounds, **T** is Tricky,
Vowel Color Chart, Transcriptions, Invisible Consonants

CHAPTER TWO — So You Want to Speak ***Engwish*** 79

The Sounds of Words

Syllables, **Stress**, The Power of the Stressed Syllable, 80% Rule,
The Page that Doesn't Matter, Stress in a Nutshell,
Schwa, Schwa in Slow Motion, Ellipse, Disappearing Syllables

CHAPTER THREE — Not All Words are Created Equally 107

The Sounds of Sentences

Content Words/Important Words, Function Words/Unimportant Words,
Similes, The Natural Rhythm of English *Speaking*,
The Best of Whatever You Are, ta da DAH, In Case They Ask, Pausing,
Review of Part One: Content Words Make History, The Future of Writing

PART TWO

ADVANCED

CHAPTER FOUR — Words Don't Begin with Vowels 139

Linking

Mumbling, Linking, Consonant to Consonant, C•C, Consonant to Vowel, C•V, Vowel to Vowel, V•V, Juan and Don, Sentence Surgery, Perfectly Good English, Fun with English, Who Cares?

CHAPTER FIVE — Words Come in Groups 163

Expressions or Collocations

Context, Words Come in Groups, Anticipation, **Collocations**, The Most Important Page in the Book, English is Abstract, Jokes and Riddles, English is Idiomatic, The Tip of the Iceberg, Fun With Collocations, Real English, Home Study

CHAPTER SIX — Non-Verbal Communication 193

Body Language

Voice Sounds and Body Language, Notes, Yes/No Questions, Tone of Voice Body Language, Gestures, Strategies, Some People Are Nasty, Smile

CONCLUSION 214

Written English and *Spoken* English are Different (Chart), Six Elements Define *Spoken* English, **English is Crazy** is the Context for *Speaking* English, Books Don't Teach New Skills

POSTSCRIPT — Tomorrow's English 218

APPENDICES 221

A Brief History of the English Language, Different Ways to Spell the Same Consonant Sound, Silent Consonants, Different Ways to Spell the Same Vowel Sound, Global English Outline for Native Speakers

REFERENCES — Books, Media and Web 229

Preface

When I started out teaching English as a Second Language (ESL), I had a vague notion that English has a few idiosyncrasies (like eight and ate, or that match could be a noun, a verb or an adjective.) With a degree in English and a college certificate in teaching ESL, I was aware that English could be tricky. But standing before my first nightschool class, teaching my first lesson, I was appalled to discover what a truly incomprehensible language English is.

There I was, full of good intentions, committed to making a difference, armed with grammar exercises, staring out at a melting pot of adult immigrants. In big, tidy letters, I began printing the verb **to be** on the blackboard:

> I am
> you are
> he is

I thought it would be a good idea to pronounce the words as I wrote them. **And I couldn't do it!** I could not pronounce I am exactly as it was printed. The way I normally say these words did not match the letters I was putting on the board. I listened to myself say:

> I yam
> you ware
> he yiz...

What the heck was that?

Then I tried producing the letters as *written*, and I sounded like I had marbles in my mouth. Nothing in forty years of using English had prepared me for the harsh reality – there is something inherently *wrong* with this language. It's crazy! Letters don't represent sounds. *Speaking* English and *writing* English are **not** the same, and the alphabet doesn't connect them. I realized that my students could not, with any measure of confidence, decipher what English sounds like by reading it. I proceeded with the class on very shaky ground. It was four years before I understood the ramifications of that first night and thousands of hours of teaching before I knew what to do about it.

Motherhood was my first career, and raising horses was my second. Both of these professions involve a great deal of communicating with creatures that don't speak English. Far more than formal training, they prepared me for my third career, which was teaching ESL. Communicating without words is how a mother understands her baby when he gurgles or how a horseman encourages a filly to walk quietly at the end of a lead rope. The purest form of communication is simply the desire to communicate. What gets in the way of communication is language, and I came to learn that the English language is the greatest obstacle of all.

Grammar has been the cornerstone of language-teaching programs. One limitation with it is the linear quality of grammar – a rule like adjectives describe nouns doesn't accommodate the abstract nature of English or what is implied by a blue moon. Subsequently, learners become so self-conscious about making grammatical errors, they are reluctant to speak at all. While grammar helps students with basic *writing* skills, studying grammar actually inhibits their ability to converse. We teach grammar, not because it works, but because it is easy to mark.

When a family immigrates to North America, the children are enrolled in public school, and the parents come to adult ESL classes. Typically, within eleven months, the children are fluent in English. In my first ten years teaching adults, **not one** student graduated fluent in English from my school. When I mentioned this to my boss, she told me if I didn't like the way they did things at the school, there were plenty of qualified teachers waiting to replace me. This is exactly what I am talking about. She didn't use the words, Shut up or you're fired, but that was what she was saying. English really is tricky.

The turning point in my career – my whole life, really – was *pronunciation*. I took a course with Kathryn Brillinger and taught a pronunciation course with Lydia Aiello. I learned hundreds of technical things about *how* English is spoken and, for me, some absolute essentials – the *must knows* of oral communication – bubbled to the surface. Over the next few years, I identified six fundamental patterns of *spoken* English that have nothing to do with the alphabet, spelling or grammar. No one is understood in English without them. Native English speakers don't teach them because first language rules operate below our level of awareness.

Working in South Korea in 2002 and had the opportunity to design a course for *speaking* English. The South Koreans already knew more grammar than I did and could spell better, too. What they wanted was to learn how to speak. My world would never be the same. I began developing the approach found in this book, starting with the **English Phonetic Alphabet** (not the Latin one that has been confusing everyone) and covering how stress works and how words work in small fixed groups to convey images.

Preface

When I came back to Canada, I was immediately hired by Sheridan College to teach my own language course to immigrant graduate students. It was called *Speaking Canadian English*. The students were amazed with their results compared to traditional methods. **Why didn't anyone tell me this before?** they cried. All they really wanted was to sound more like native speakers, to express themselves in their new country, to make friends. My students learned that English isn't a sound-based language (Chapter Two.) Gone were their concerns about their accents when they learned accents don't affect intelligibility. They realized that there are *important* words and *unimportant* words (Chapter Three), and they could listen faster and not fret so much about grammar. They learned about body language and tone of voice as tools for communication. Then they quit school. My students went out in the world, volunteered in their communities, got jobs and made friends. The world became their classroom. There was no conversation they couldn't manage and no idea they couldn't express.

As an ESL teacher, the most powerful gift I can give my students is confidence. I have been able to do that by clearly distinguishing between *written* English and *spoken* English. The elements of *spoken* English outlined in this book are what students need to set out on a successful path to *speaking*. When students understand the *six patterns* of how English *speaking* really works, they realize that they don't have to be perfect to communicate. It sets them free. Sure they make mistakes, but they aren't stopped by them. In the global community, I trust their efforts will be met halfway where no one has to be perfect to be understood. The simple desire to communicate with each other transcends any language obstacle.

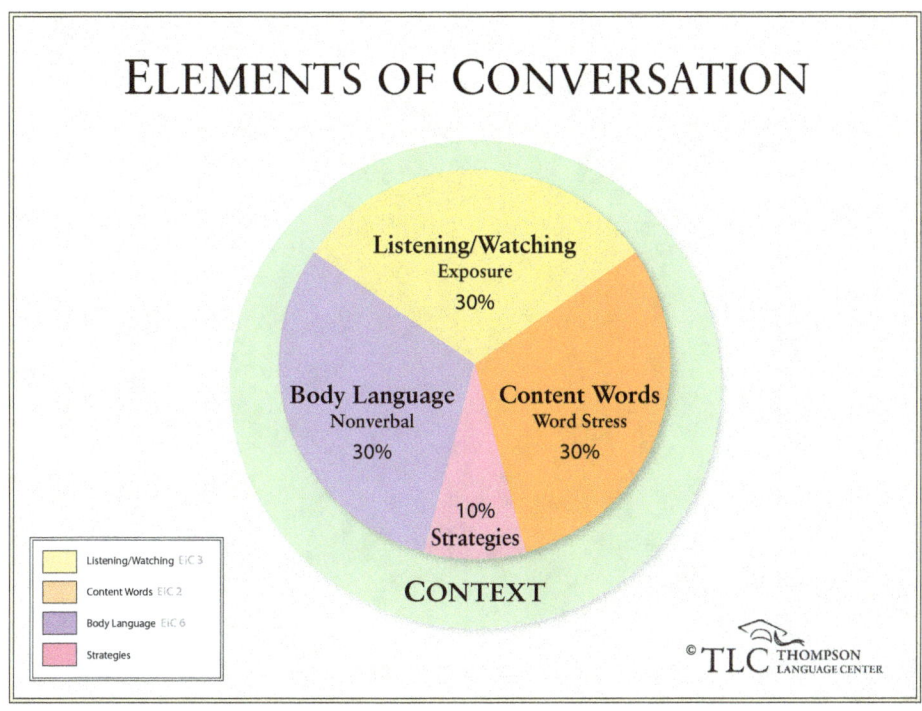

Introduction

Great Britain rose to power on the world stage in 1588 with the defeat of the Spanish Armada and her magnificent fleet of tall ships. Britain's dominance continued for many centuries in many fields. In 1684, Sir Isaac Newton published *Principia* and ushered in industrialization and a new era in modern science. Britain reigned as a world leader for nearly four hundred years and left the stamp of English around the globe. In 1945 at the end of World War II, her authority passed directly to the United States of America. These two back-to-back superpowers happened to share a common language. Between them, they effectively established English as the global *lingua franca*.

Of the 2 billion people using English today, the vast majority are not native speakers. English learners outnumber native speakers by a margin of 5:1.

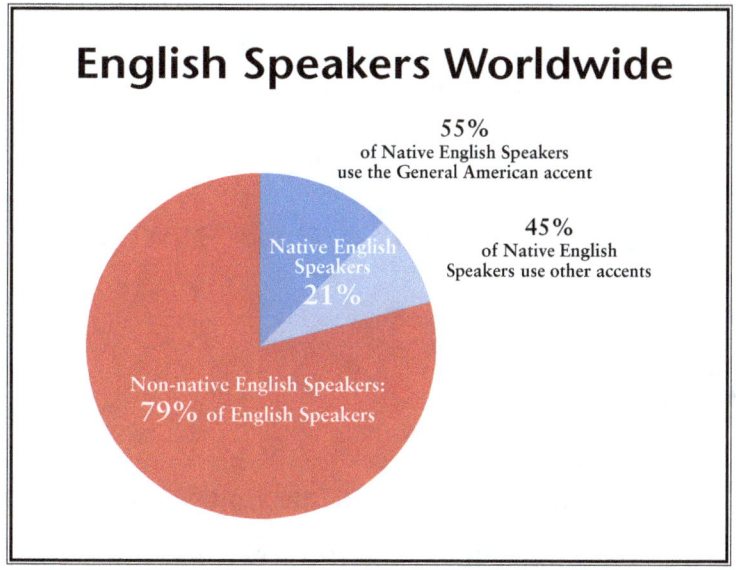

Over a billion people are currently learning English and to date, there hasn't been an effective way to teach it. This ends here. The General American (GA) aka Hollywood accent is the accent featured in *English is Crazy*. 70% of the 380 million native English speakers worldwide use GA. It is naturally the accent most sought-after by learners.

Students who study English in school learn primarily about *reading* and *writing* and are frustrated that the *speaking* doesn't follow. The fly in the ointment is the Latin alphabet.

The heart of our trouble is with our foolish alphabet.
Mark Twain

Introduction

There is no crossover from *written* English to *spoken* English through the alphabet. Therefore, **no one can learn to speak English from reading it.** In effect, *written* English and *spoken* English developed separately into completely different languages and must be taught that way for students to be successful. Traditionally, the grammar, spelling, punctuation and reading skills taught in language classes are all about *writing* and simply do not relate in any meaningful way to the mumbling, grunting, inflection, pausing and gestures that somehow work together to make conversation.

Think back to how you learned your first language. Human beings acquire their first language as toddlers. They learn to speak by mimicking those around them. There is no formal understanding of the mechanics of any language in order to speak it. The patterns are acquired subconsciously. Conversely, grammar and spelling are parts of language studied in school sometime after the age of six. Mastery of grammar comes most effectively from using a language *not* from reading about it.

First language skills are acquired in this order:

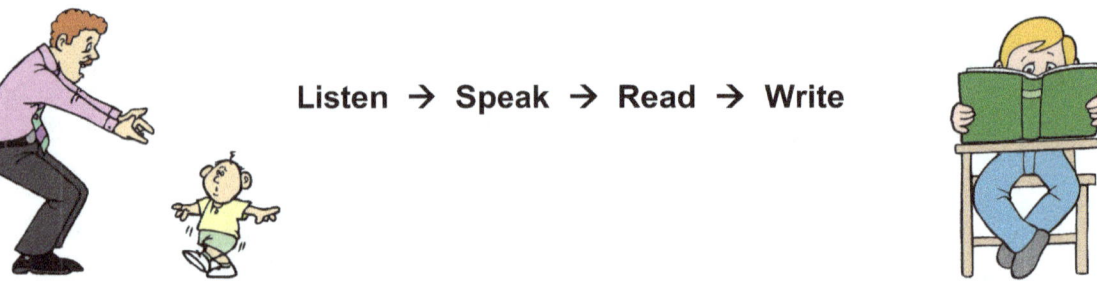

Listen → Speak → Read → Write

English has no clear-cut relationship between the alphabet and sounds; therefore, the **language learning process cannot be reversed**. No one can learn to read and write English and expect *speaking* English to follow because the skills are unconnected.

A specialized approach is required to unlock how English conversation works. That's what this book is about. *Speaking* **is not simply** *writing* **spoken out loud**. *Speaking* and *writing* are different skills that use different sets of rules. The simple set of six patterns in this book addresses all aspects of oral communication. A clear understanding of the distinctions between *writing* and *speaking* provides a powerful place for learners to stand.

Reading and *Writing*   *Speaking* and *Listening*

USE Eyes	USE Hands	USE Mouths	USE Ears

			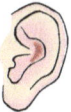

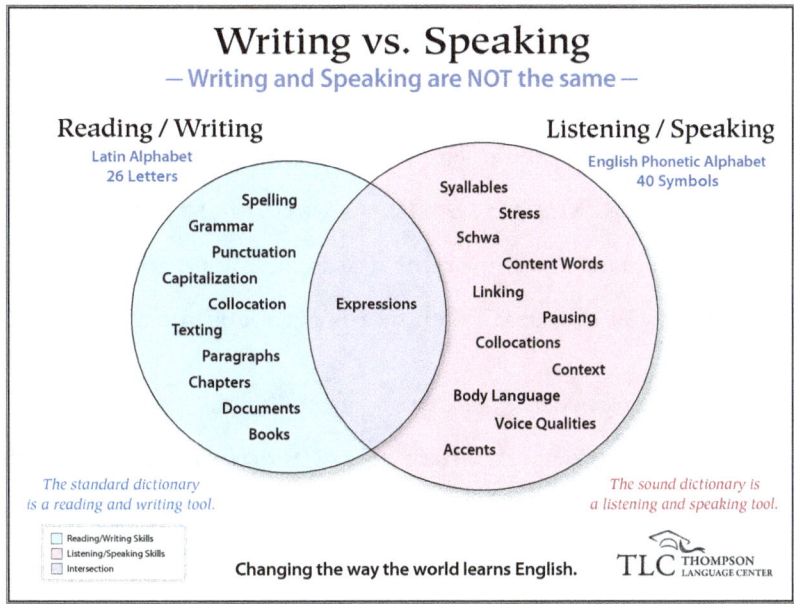

Reading
- alphabet
- spelling
- punctuation
- format
- grammar

Speaking
- sounds
- stress
- linking
- expressions
- gestures

Writing and *speaking* are different language skills, and they have to be taught with separate rules. *Spoken* English is defined by a set of **six** very simple principles outlined in this book that will set the student on the right track to *speaking* fluently.

Introduction

Guide for *Spoken* English

Phonetic Alphabet: English spelling is random. Students need a functional **sound alphabet** for *speaking* that identifies the 40 sound units of English and complements the *writing* alphabet. The *English Phonetic Alphabet* (EPA) is a simple, student-friendly sound alphabet using standard keyboard symbols.

Stress-based Language: Although it is good to know *about* the sounds of English, it is not necessary to recreate them all perfectly. The meaning in English is not in individual sounds but in word stress. **English is a stress-based language**. Students need to listen for *word stress* in native English speaking and be able to create *word stress* when they talk.

Important Words: In many spoken languages, each syllable in every word is equally important. Not in English. **Native speakers enunciate only important words**. They slur over or eliminate less important words, creating more or less a rhythm when they speak. Students need to know which words get focus and which are reduced.

Linking: Slurred native speech is often unintelligible, even to native speakers. Thankfully, **English words are slurred in predictable places by a process called Linking**. Understanding this helps students in two ways. They can decode what is being said to them, and they can produce their own native-like speech.

Collocations: English is typically taught in word units labelled as parts of speech, but it is not used that way. **English comes in thousands of small fixed word groups called collocations** that are not necessarily literal or logical. English is idiomatic, using set groups of words and **expressions** to convey ideas. Alone, words have little meaning and are defined by the **context** in which they occur.

Body Language: Beyond the first five aspects, **English speakers communicate non-verbally**. In English, body language, **gesturing**, pausing, intonation and tone of voice are tools far more powerful than words.

This book is designed with separate sections for teachers and students to work side by side through the six chapters to unravel the mysteries of *spoken* English.

© Judy Thompson 2009

Teacher Introduction

Generally, vocabulary is the knowledge of meanings of words. What complicates this definition is the fact that words come in at least two forms: oral and print.   Elfrieda H. Hiebert, Michael L. Kamil

What to Do?

There is a separate method for learning to *speak* English compared to *writing* it.

To learn to speak English, ESL students must do four things:

1) **Listen** 👂

   Students have to listen to *hundreds of hours* of English without necessarily understanding what is being said. Students need to listen to English outside the classroom. Recommend strategies. Students can watch soap operas on television – the characters don't change and the plot is slow. Have them leave radios, podcasts, books on tape and interviews in English on all the time and watch the same Netflix shows over and over again. The first time they watch a movie, they may understand 20%; the fourth time, 80%. Inside the classroom – repeat, repeat, repeat. (Then there are some things they only have to hear once…)

   In order to speak, students have to absorb the basic sounds of the language by being exposed to hundreds of hours of listening – exactly as they learned their first language.

2) **Learn**

   Students must learn the patterns of the *speaking* game – the **six patterns of oral communication** found in this book.

   - **Sound Alphabet**
   - **Word Stress**
   - **Important Words**
   - **Linking**
   - **Expressions**
   - **Body Language**

All Germans speak English with a German accent, all Chinese with a Chinese accent... The patterns that shape each spoken language operate beneath a speaker's level of awareness. This book reveals the precepts for *spoken* English. When students understand how English works, they can make English choices to override the programming of their first language. Learners can't choose English if they don't know how English compares with their first language.

3) Think

In the flow of conversation, speakers constantly assimilate information from education, experiences, context, culture, vocabulary, and gestures. There is little in the study of reading or writing that prepares students for speaking. It helps learners when instructors separate writing and speaking on the board. **Writing** on the left in black and **Speaking** on the right in red.

4) Practice

It's not easy. It takes courage to speak another language. For learners, understanding native speakers is nearly impossible, and trying to join a casual conversation takes the same amount of courage as jumping out of an airplane.

Because *speaking* doesn't match up with the *writing* or vocabulary they have learned, conversation is always a guessing game for students.

Students need to know that English is a guessing game for native speakers, too — no one is 100% sure what anyone is saying. This is how politicians get elected. Misunderstanding is a problem in English, not just an ESL problem. *Speaking* English is like a game.

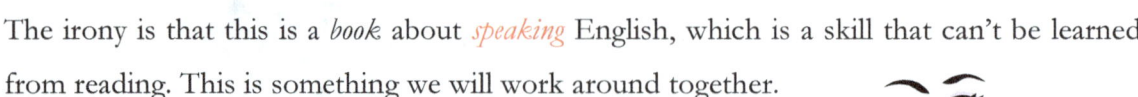

The irony is that this is a *book* about *speaking* English, which is a skill that can't be learned from reading. This is something we will work around together.

English Conversation is a Game Called

What Do You Think They Said?

Anyone with teenagers has heard *bad hair day* and *Therez nuthin t'eat* and wondered, *I think he was speaking English, but I have no idea what he just said.* English is not explicit or literal; it's **abstract** and **implied**. Native speakers slur and mumble and struggle to understand each other. In conversation, native English speakers take into account an array of *signals* in a fraction of a second – and then guess. Context drives conversation not grammar. *English is Crazy* takes a close look at the *elements* that make up messages. Good communicators are, in fact, confident guessers. ESL students should know that *speaking* **English is a guessing game**. Have some fun with it.

When your son asks, *Whadaya doin' tonight?*,

He wants to borrow the car.

When a mechanic says, *I hafta replace the head gasket.*

It's going to be expensive.

When an actor on the silver screen says, *Tell her the cool points are all out the window and she's got me all twisted up in the game*[1],

He's in love.

Students need to understand that nobody understands English perfectly.

Everybody guesses!

---

[1] Eugene Levy in *Bringing Down the House*

But...

When native speakers don't understand something, they just say, **What?**  But they are not ashamed.

When ESL students are unsure of what's been said,  they feel humiliated and blame their *poor* English.

The sooner they find out how English *speaking* works and that English is imprecise and everybody just guesses, the happier and more confident they are going to feel.

Students are not stupid.   **English is crazy!**

Students are embarrassed when they try to speak English because of their accents and grammar. They are afraid of looking foolish. The truth is, accents and grammar play no part in successful English communication – so their worries are not real. **English is Crazy** explores the **six patterns** of *spoken* English (as distinct from *written* English.) With this tiny bit of insight, students are empowered and free to communicate in their new language.

Student Workbook Introduction

English looks like this:

Roses are red,
Violets are blue,
Sugar is sweet
And so are you.

English sounds like this:

roziz ar red
vilets ar bluw
shuger iz sweet
an so ar yuw

one
wun

house
haws

boat
bowt

clock
klok

sugar
shuger

face
fays

eyes
iyz

orange
orenj

school
skuwl

What to Do!

OK, so English is crazy. English *speaking* and English *writing* are not the same. What can you do? To *speak* English, students must do **four** things:

1) **Listen** to hours and hours of English.

    YouTube   Podcasts   Movies & Videos   Conversations

2) **Learn** the rules of *spoken* English.

3) **Think** about the context of the conversation and understand speaking doesn't work like the English studied in school.

    books   talking

4) **Practice** *speaking* English.

It's not easy.

The more you do it,

the easier it gets.

It's going to be all right.

HOW THIS BOOK WORKS

Teacher Page

There is one chapter in this book for each of the **six** essential patterns of *spoken* English.

Part One: Chapters One to **Three**, BASIC, separates *speaking* from *writing* English. Learning to speak English is like learning English all over again, from the beginning, including the sounds of letters, words and sentences.

Part Two: Chapters Four to **Six**, ADVANCED, addresses the leap from the elementary to the abstract elements of the English language. English is idiomatic, and not all languages are. Part Two includes linking, expressions and non-verbal communication.

Layout

Throughout the body of the textbook, the ***Teacher's Guide*** is printed on the left-hand side in Garamond font with a lined border. The Teacher's Guide includes a more complete account of the material to be used at the teacher's discretion, including historical anecdotes, lesson ideas and answer keys.

On the right-hand side is the **Student Workbook** in Arial font. The Student Workbook includes a pictorial explanation of the principles and a variety of exercises for students, beginner to advanced levels. Naturally, students are going to peek at the teacher's side. There is good information there, so if they can understand it – more power to them.

In each chapter:

- There is a lesson on one basic pattern of *speaking*.
- There are exercises on the students' pages to practice the point. The exercises gradually increase in difficulty – beginner, intermediate and advanced.
- Finally, there is a laundry list at the end summarizing the highlights this chapter.

It is critical for English learners to be aware of the disconnect between written and spoken English and to understand the six patterns that govern how native English speakers converse. More than anything, when students get the distinction between how English is *spoken* from how English is *written,* they are filled with confidence, and their bold *speaking* journey can begin.

HOW THIS BOOK WORKS

Part One: Beginner

1	Letters	ABC	
	English Phonetic Alphabet	Ay bEy sEy	
2	Words		
	Stressed Syllables	ba **NA** na	
3	Sentences		
	Important Words	a **CUP** a **COFFEE**	

Part Two: Advanced

4	Word Breaks		
	Linking	Ca nI ha va bi da **vegg**?	
5	Abstract English		
	Expressions	When pigs fly!	
6	Non-verbal Communication		
	Body Language	Smile	

Left Side   **Right Side**
Teacher Guide   **Student Workbook**

Lessons   Lessons

Information   Examples

Answer Keys   Exercises

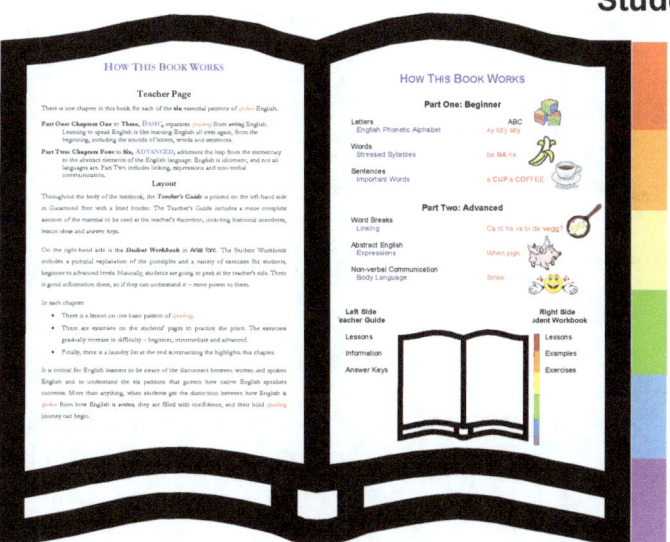

Have fun!

www.thompsonlanguagecenter.com

Legend

 **Teacher Pages:** Left-hand pages

Student Pages: Right-hand pages

Brown Colored Text **Quotes and Related Information**

[Green Colored Text]. **Stage Directions**

 **Book within a Book:** Pink border
English Phonetic Alphabet

 **Answer Key:** To the student exercise on the previous page

 **Lesson Ideas:** Teacher pages

Thompson Language Center YouTube Channel
for the PLAYLIST *Judy Thompson Teaching Speaking*

 **Jokes:** Native speakers think these are funny.

 **Exceptions:** There are exceptions to every rule.

 **Unlock the Secrets:** A summary of what is most important for students to know at the end of each chapter

 **Laundry List:**   Chapter summary

Part One

BASIC

Letters – Phonetic Alphabet

Words – Stressed Syllables

Sentences – Important Words

Chapter One

LETTERS

Spelling is Random

The traditional alphabet consists of nothing whatever except silliness.
Mark Twain

CHAPTER ONE

Spelling is Random

ABC is the *Latin* alphabet. English doesn't have an alphabet. The Latin alphabet was inadvertently left in Britain by the fleeing Romans over fifteen hundred years ago and has caused no end of trouble ever since. Specifically, the symbols A to Z do not correspond to English language sounds. An alphabet that doesn't represent the sounds of the language is a devastating concept for students learning to speak. Over time, with no alphabet to unify the sounds and symbols of the language, *spoken* English and *written* English have evolved into two completely different languages.

Ancient History [2]

Spelling has never worked in English. In the olden days, the alphabet was like a secret code that gave mystical powers to the few who could make sense of it. When William Caxton set up his printing press in 1476, spelling was as individual as the writer dipping his quill. For the first one hundred years of the printing industry, typesetters were more concerned with symmetry than consistency, and they added and subtracted letters to justify their margins. A sense grew among the educated and literate that spelling should be standardized, so the industry began moving in that direction. The first dictionary was printed in 1603; by the mid 1600s, inconsistent spelling was frowned upon. Not much has changed in the *written* language since 1700, which is a damn shame because it has so very little to do with how the language is spoken.

One Alphabet

Scholars and visionaries, rankled at the disparity between the English sound and spelling, began to think of solutions. Famous and influential Americans like Theodore Roosevelt and Dale Carnegie spoke out against the fallacious alphabet and rallied to fix the problem. Mark Twain developed a simplified alphabet, and Isaac Pitman devised **shorthand**, but no remedy widely caught on. Special phonetic alphabets were composed that united sounds and symbols, to no avail. The public resisted change. People were reluctant to depart from their familiar Latin characters and remained true to the dysfunctional Latin alphabet. The cost of using the Latin alphabet for English is staggering.

> *Statistically, more American children suffer long-term life harm from the process of learning to read than from parental abuse, accidents, and all other childhood diseases and disorders combined. In purely economic terms, reading-related difficulties cost our nation more than the war on terrorism, crime, and drugs* ***combined***.
> Children of the Code

What Can Be Done?

The first thing that ESL students need to understand is that *spoken* English is in no way represented by *written* English. The second thing they need is a **sound alphabet**. *Speaking* begins when students can *hear* the words they *read*.

---

[2] See Appendix 1, A Brief History of the English Language

The Sounds of Letters

Big English Problem: Letters ≠ Sounds

Writing uses the Latin alphabet.

Speaking uses ?

English *speaking* needs a *special* alphabet – one *symbol* for every *sound*.

Speaking uses sounds.

Sounds are *blocks* for language.
/bloks/

They make a *foundation*.
/fawndayshun/

The 40 sounds of English are the *foundation* of *spoken* English.

English has **two** types of sounds – **consonant** sounds and **vowel** sounds.

There are **24 consonant** sounds
+ <u>**16** **vowel**</u> sounds
40 sounds in English

and only 26 letters in the Latin alphabet!

Teacher Page　　　　　　　　　　Letters

Recipe for an *English* Alphabet

1. Ingredients – ordinary computer keyboard symbols
2. Amounts – 40 symbols, one for each sound
3. Presentation – letters suggest the sounds they represent

A brand new, easy to use, logical, Latin-alphabet-based **English Phonetic Alphabet** has been cooked up!

The Alphabet Story Continued…

In 1888, a solution for the alphabet problem was developed. Use two separate alphabets. The Latin alphabet remained for *written* English, and another alphabet was devised for *speaking*. The International Phonetic Alphabet (IPA) from Paris is a huge bank of phonetic (sound) symbols, one for every sound produced in all major languages. With IPA, any language could draw the symbols for the sounds it uses from one standard set of symbols. It was a great idea.

IPA uses many of the Latin characters English speakers are familiar with and added new symbols to represent sounds like **sh** as in <u>sh</u>in / ʃ/, and **ch** as in <u>ch</u>in /tʃ/, and **th** as in <u>th</u>in /θ/. IPA is the **pronunciation** alphabet used in many dictionaries.

The drawbacks of the International Phonetic Alphabet for English were twofold: The new symbols like /dʒ/ were too obscure to bother with, and letters that clearly represented one sound in English were chosen to represent different sounds in IPA. For example, the letter **j** was chosen to represent the sound /y/. In IPA, **jellow** was a color not a food. It was far too confusing. One confusing system was replaced by another. The International Phonetic Alphabet is a wonderful concept but not an effective solution for English.

Teacher Note

The Latin alphabet is familiar to students – like an old friend.

When ABC gets relegated to *writing* only, it leaves a void that can make students anxious. The remedy is to fill the void at once with a substitute that works for them. Students fall in love instantly with the **English Phonetic Alphabet** (EPA) because it is a 100% reliable representation of the sounds they hear. Uniting letters and sounds is fun. The effort to learn the EPA is repaid immediately and a hundred times over. It's a solid foundation.

Like the foundation in your house, it's worth investing in a good one.

STUDY CONSONANTS FOR ONE WEEK AND VOWELS FOR TWO.

© Judy Thompson 2009

Student Page

THE ENGLISH PHONETIC ALPHABET

The *English Phonetic Alphabet* is for *speaking*.
It is a **phonetic** or **sound** alphabet.
funedik   alfabet

Learning a new alphabet is really, really boring,
but it's your foundation for *speaking* English.
If you don't make a good foundation …

your **house** will fall down.
/hAws/

Rule #1   Letters don't represent sounds.

If you <u>really</u> understand this and you know a good phonetic alphabet,
skip right to Chapter Two. If not, read on.

The English Phonetic Alphabet

Speaking symbols are printed between slanted lines / /   to show **sound**.

For example:

dog

Woof

This is a **dog**.   It makes the *sound* **/woof/**

This is a **d**.   It makes the *sound* **/d/** as in <u>d</u>og.

This is an **m**.   It makes the *sound* **/m/** as in <u>m</u>oon.

You have to *hear* the words when you *read* them. To do that, you need a new

alphabet. The **English Phonetic Alphabet** is a bridge to *speaking* English.

Reading

Speaking

www.thompsonlanguagecenter.com   33

Teacher Page English Phonetic Alphabet

Consonant Sounds

There are **24** consonant sounds in English. Consonants are **stopped** or restricted sounds. [Stage directions – chop your right hand onto the palm of your left in an emphatic motion with each sound – /b/, /d/, /f/ – finished or stopped sounds.] Students will get the idea.

The consonant sounds in the **English Phonetic Alphabet** are featured on the next page. *Capital* and underlined letters indicate sounds represented by pairs of symbols. ⇨

FYI

This is not a pronunciation textbook. It showcases the 40 sounds of the General American (GA) accent using standard keyboard symbols. Also known as a *Hollywood accent*, more than half of all native English speakers globally use GA and it is the most widely sought accent by learners

It is important for learners to know that meaning in English is NOT in the perfect production of individual sounds. English is NOT a sound-based language. Spoken English tolerates infinite sound variations, substitutions, and omissions. Intelligibility in English is in Chapter Two.

Sister Sounds

Pairs of sounds that are formed in exactly the same place in the mouth are **sister sounds**. It is useful to know. One **sister** is made by blowing air out from the mouth in a given position, and its **sister** is made by drawing air *in* from the same mouth position, creating a sound from the throat.

Air Out		Air In	
/p/	pig	/b/	big
/t/	to	/d/	do
/k/	came	/g/	game
/f/	fan	/v/	van
/s/	said	/z/	zed
/TH/ [1]	thigh	/Th/	thy
/ch/	cheap	/j/	jeep
/sh/	shone	/zh/	genre

Lesson Idea

Minimal Pair Exercises: pat/bat, time/dime, chin/gin...
[Stage directions – For fun, hold a piece of paper in front of your lips and say "pig, pen, pat, thigh, thin, thank…" It will move for /p/, /t/, /k/…]

---

[1] Capital letters indicate a pair of symbols is representing one sound.

© Judy Thompson, 2009

ENGLISH PHONETIC ALPHABET (EPA)

iNgliSh   funedik   alfabet

24 Consonant Sounds

18 Symbols you know

EPA Symbol	Key Word	EPA Symbol	Key Word
/b/	**b**oy	/n/	**n**umber
/d/	**d**og	/p/	**p**eople
/f/	**f**ive	/r/	**r**ed
/g/	**g**oat	/s/	**s**ummer
/h/	**h**ouse	/t/	**t**ime
/j/	**J**uly	/v/	**v**isa
/k/	**k**ing	/w/	**w**oman
/l/	**l**emon	/y/	**y**ellow
/m/	**m**oney	/z/	**z**ebra

+ 6 New symbols

EPA Symbol	Key Word
/Sh/	**sh**oe
/Ch/	**ch**urch
/TH/	**th**ink (tongue between your teeth and **blow air out**)
/Th/	**th**en (tongue between your teeth and **suck air in**)
/Ng/	Ho**ng** Ko**ng**
/zh/	A**s**ia, bei**g**e, televi**s**ion (there is no English letter for /zh/)

= 24 Consonant sounds

Beware of **Silent Consonants** – They make no sound. They are everywhere!

thum**b**, wa**l**k, **k**nife, ans**w**er, **w**rite

ø is the symbol when a letter is silent.

Teacher Page English Phonetic Alphabet

Baby Beginner Quiz

Working in pairs is a great way to get students to practice listening and speaking – double bang for the buck! If the students correct each other, congratulations! It is a sign of a **safe** classroom environment.

Yankee
According to the Oxford English Dictionary, *Yankee* is derived from the Dutch surnames **Jan** and **Kees**. **Jan** means **John** and may have been used as a form of contempt in addressing Dutch settlers in New York. By extension, the term grew to include non-Dutch American colonists as well. Now, the term carries less emotion – except, of course, for baseball fans.

Canada
Kanata! young Indian braves shouted as they pointed towards home upon returning from France with Jacques Cartier. The boys meant **village**, but Cartier misheard the **t** for its sister sound **d**, and this land has been called Canada ever since.

Teacher Talk

English is a Language of Exceptions

Every time you think you have a great rule, you find an exception. For students, **usually** is close enough. Too many details bog them down. They need the patterns that are always true. All the exercises in this text are sample exercises. They can be modified to suit any topic. Adapt the level of difficulty for each class. ***The English Phonetic Alphabet Workbook*** for Chapter One of *English is Crazy* features EPA and contains hundreds of exercises for individual sound practice (Amazon).

More sounds c can make:

    c makes the sound /Ch/ in words like c̲ello and cappuc̲c̲ino

    c makes the sound /Sh/ in words like oc̲ean, soc̲ial and delic̲ious

    c is silent /Ø/ and makes no sound in words like musc̲le, sc̲ience and sc̲issors

Why? Because **English is crazy**.

Technically, there is no such thing as a **c** sound, and that is why it got kicked out of the phonetic alphabet – it's useless.

© Judy Thompson 2009

English Phonetic Alphabet   Student Page

Super Easy Baby Beginner Quiz

Put the sound of the underlined letter in the brackets beside the word. / /

do<u>g</u> / g /   <u>y</u>ellow / /   <u>th</u>ink / /

<u>v</u>est / /   <u>k</u>nife / /   <u>ch</u>air / /

<u>sh</u>oes / /   <u>h</u>orse / /   ki<u>ng</u> / /

<u>z</u>ipper / /   mo<u>th</u>er / /   com<u>b</u> / /

There. **Easy**. The consonant sounds of English.

There are 24 consonants in the **English Phonetic Alphabet.**

- **18 familiar symbols** that sound like they look
    (We are not doing vowels now.)

  a b c̶ d e f g h i j k l m n o p q̶ r s t u v w x̶ y z
  /b/ /d/   /f/ /g/ /h/ /j/ /k/ /l/ /m/ /n/   /p/   /r/ /s/ /t/   /v/ /w/   /y/ /z/

- **6 new symbols**

    /ch/ - church   /TH/ - think   /NG/ - ring
    /sh/ - shoe   /TH/ - the   /zh/ - Asia

  and ø when the letter is silent

There is no **c**, **q** or **x** in the phonetic alphabet.

    c usually makes the sound   /s/ as in <u>c</u>ity
                                  or   /k/ as in <u>c</u>at
    q usually makes the sound   /kw/ as in <u>qu</u>een
    x usually makes the sound   /eks/ as in <u>x</u>-ray

www.thompsonlanguagecenter.com

Teacher Page   English Phonetic Alphabet

Chose a New Path

To speak English, students have to start down a new path that includes a sound alphabet and listening, listening, listening. If students *really* understand that, then go on to **Chapter Two**.

Listening is the path to *speaking* English, not **reading**.

But don't put down this book!

English is Crazy showcases the *patterns* of *speaking* and lots of cool information.

I hold that a man has just as mutch rite tew spel a word as it is pronounced, as he has tew pronounce it the way it ain't spelt.

Chastity iz like an isikel; if it onse melts, that's the last of it.
           Josh Billings (1818 – 1885), an American writer renowned for his **phonetic** and **prophetic** work.

Sounds g can make:

     g makes the sound /j/ in words like giant and gym

     g makes the sound /f/ in words like lau<u>gh</u> and cou<u>gh</u>

     g makes the sound /zh/ in words like genre, beige and garage

     g makes the sound /p/ in the word hiccou<u>gh</u>

     g makes no sound at all in words like sight and though

Answer Key 🗝

Super Baby Beginner Easy Quiz

<u>d</u>og /g/   <u>y</u>ellow /y/   <u>th</u>ink /TH/   <u>v</u>est /v/   <u>k</u>nife /Ø/   <u>ch</u>air /Ch/

<u>sh</u>oe /sh/   <u>h</u>orse /h/   ki<u>ng</u> /Ng/   <u>z</u>ipper /z/   mo<u>th</u>er /Th/   com<u>b</u> /Ø/

© Judy Thompson 2009

English Phonetic Alphabet   Student Page

The Problem with Consonants

kake

jentelman

unyunz

klowz

Spelled: **cake, gentleman
onion, clothes**

One problem with consonants is that the same letter can represent so many different sounds. **Words don't sound like they look**.[4] Every letter in English can represent more than one sound or be silent at any time. There are no rules. We already talked about **c**. Let's try another – how about **g**:

Usually,
> **g** makes the sound /g/ as in good, girl, game, get

Sometimes,
> **g** makes the sound /j/ as in giant, giraffe, gymnastics

Sometimes,
> **g** is silent, /ø/ as in sign, gnat, foreign, though

c and **g** are not the only problems. The list goes on and on… **t** is the worst. On page 43, you'll find a special section about the letter **t** after a little practice exercise.

cc and **gg** are the only double consonants where each can make a different sound: access/akses/ and suggest/sugjest/. Other double consonants are pronounced as one sound.

---

[4] See Appendix 2 – Different Ways to Spell the Same Consonant Sound

Teacher Page   English Phonetic Alphabet

Consonant Hunt

Have the students read the exercises on the opposite page out loud. Beginner students should read to their partners, and advanced students to themselves – but always out loud.

Students and their First Language

Students don't have trouble creating most individual English consonants. Sometimes, different languages lack specific sounds. For example, South Asians may pronounce **w** as /v/ so the day after Tuesday becomes *Vensday*. French speakers may pronounce **th** as /d/ and say, De weader is sunny. Substitutions are generally considered charming and do not impede communication. Consonants are a big problem because they are poorly represented by the Latin alphabet, not because they can't be pronounced.

All Chinese speak English with a Chinese accent, all Spanish speak English with a Spanish accent, all Germans speak English with a German accent… First language software is powerful. Students of English have to override their first language that taught them that letters represent sounds. Students will sort out words and meanings once they have been set on the right track. The Latin letter system isn't going to help them speak English, so supply them with a functional phonetic alphabet. It's a solution that works.

Hidden Treasure

Students may recognize that some of the words in the following exercises have been used in this text before. Good. If they ask about a word they have seen before, don't tell them – let them look things up.

Lesson Idea

This is a great time for a lesson on plurals and/or the simple present.

There are three sounds **s** makes at the end of a word.

The **s** ending sounds like /s/, /z/ or /iz/.

    cat**s** dog**s**   dresse**s**
    /s/   /z/   /iz/

Plural S Flashcards PDF (26 cards) available as a free download from **www.ThompsonLanguageCenter.com**

© Judy Thompson 2009

English Phonetic Alphabet   Student Page

Consonant Hunt

Put the sound of the underlined letter in the brackets beside the word / /.

Intermediate   Examples: <u>c</u>at /k/
                                <u>ph</u>one /f/   *Hint: Read the words out loud.*

<u>c</u>ity / /   <u>q</u>uarter / /   A<u>s</u>ia / /   bei<u>g</u>e / /

s<u>ch</u>ool / /   <u>k</u>nee / /   <u>h</u>our / /   wa<u>l</u>k / /

<u>w</u>rite / /   <u>z</u>oo / /   me<u>l</u>on / /   ba<u>ck</u> / /

<u>s</u>ugar / /   pen<u>s</u> / /   si<u>ng</u> / /   <u>g</u>ift / /

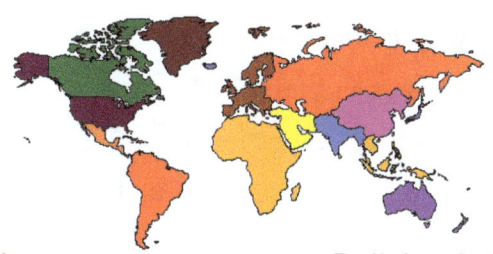

Advanced

<u>P</u>akistan / p /   <u>B</u>olivia / /

<u>T</u>hailand / t /   <u>D</u>enmark / /

<u>C</u>anada / /   <u>G</u>hana / /

<u>F</u>rance / /   <u>V</u>enezuela / /

Sou<u>th</u> Africa / /   <u>T</u>he Netherlands / /

<u>S</u>weden / /   <u>Z</u>ambia / /

<u>C</u>hina / /   <u>G</u>ermany / /

Ru<u>ss</u>ia / /   Malay<u>s</u>ia / /

<u>H</u>ungary / /   <u>L</u>ebanon / /

<u>M</u>exico / /   <u>N</u>igeria / /

<u>R</u>omania / /   <u>W</u>ales / /

<u>U</u>nited States / /   E<u>ng</u>land / /

Teacher Page   English Phonetic Alphabet

Terrible T

Student page 43 describes **nine** common things that happen with **t**. ⇨
Here are **eight** more that teachers should know:

10. At the end of a word, **t** is *unreleased* (barely said) like ½ a **t**; compare ten and ten<u>t</u>. The words *when / went* and *war / wart* sound almost the same.

11. In **front** of **ial**, **t** can sound like /ch/: essen<u>t</u>ial and substan<u>t</u>ial.

12. This is a very subtle one: **t** can sound like /ch/ in the consonant blend **tr** – <u>t</u>ruck, <u>t</u>rain

13. With an **n** in front of a **t** in an *unstressed* syllable, **t** is usually **silent**:

    i<u>n</u>ternet, fa<u>n</u>tasy and To<u>r</u>onto sound like /inernet/, /fanasy/ and /Torono/

    mi<u>nt</u>s sounds like /mince/ and pri<u>nt</u>s sounds like /prince/

    (Also true of **t**'s sister sound **d** – page 44)

14. When an **n** follows **t**, it is the same thing – a silent **t**.

    of<u>t</u>en becomes /of'en/, and mit<u>t</u>ens becomes /mi'ens/

15. There are *exceptions* where **t** is pronounced after an **n**.

    con<u>t</u>est, con<u>t</u>ent ... because English is crazy.

How English Really Sounds

16. When a word ending in **t** is followed by the word **you**, the sound is: /cha/
    Don'<u>t y</u>ou = /doncha/ Don'<u>t y</u>ou want to kiss me? /doncha wanna kiss me?/

17. When a word ending in **t** is followed by **your** or **you're**, the sound is /cher/
    Don'<u>t y</u>our = /doncher/ Don'<u>t y</u>our feet hurt? = /don<u>cher</u> feet hurt?/

Cha and **cher** are a few of the very common words that students hear every day, but they can't find 'em in the dictionary!

Answer Key 🗝

Intermediate

<u>c</u>ity /s/	<u>qu</u>arter /kw/	A<u>s</u>ia /zh/	<u>b</u>eige /zh/
s<u>ch</u>ool /k/	<u>kn</u>ee /Ø/	<u>h</u>our /Ø/	wal<u>k</u> /Ø/
<u>w</u>rite /Ø/	<u>z</u>oo /z/	me<u>l</u>on /l/	ba<u>ck</u> /k/
<u>s</u>ugar /sh/	pen<u>s</u> /z/	si<u>n</u>g /ng/	<u>g</u>ift /g/

Advanced

<u>P</u>akistan /p/	<u>B</u>olivia /b/	<u>Th</u>ailand /t/	<u>D</u>enmark /d/
<u>C</u>anada /k/	<u>Gh</u>ana /g/	<u>F</u>rance /f/	<u>V</u>enezuela /v/
Sou<u>th</u> Africa /TH/	<u>Th</u>e Netherlands /Th/	<u>S</u>weden /s/	<u>Z</u>ambia /z/
<u>Ch</u>ina /ch/	<u>G</u>ermany /j/	Ru<u>ss</u>ia /sh/	Malay<u>s</u>ia /zh/
<u>H</u>ungary /h/	<u>L</u>ebanon /l/	<u>M</u>exico /m/	<u>N</u>igeria /n/
<u>R</u>omania /r/	<u>W</u>ales /w/	United States /y/	E<u>n</u>gland /ng/

© Judy Thompson 2009

English Phonetic Alphabet   Student Page

Terrible T

Be careful of **t**. No other letter in English makes as many sounds as the letter **t**. It is usually /t/ at the beginning of a word and usually /d/ in the middle of a word, but it can be /sh/, /ch/, /j/ or silent /ø/!

1. **t** sounds like /t/ at the <u>beginning</u> of a word   tree /tree/

2. In the middle of a word, **t** is usually /d/   butter /budder/

3. **t** can be /sh/   direction /direcshun/

4. **t** can be /ch/   furniture /furnicher/

5. **t** can be /j/   question /kwesjun/

6. **t** can be silent /ø/   whistle /wisel/

7. At the <u>end</u> of a word, **t** is unreleased.   ½ /t/ – can't sounds like /can t/

8. At the <u>end</u> of a word, **ed** can be /t/   shopped /shopt/

    kissed /kist/

    laughed /laft/

9. At the <u>end</u> of a word, **et** can be /ay/   ballet /balay/

So **t** is *tricky*. Pay attention to letter **t**.

Because English is crazy.

www.thompsonlanguagecenter.com

T and D

We've talked about some of the sounds **t** can represent. Conversely, here are some letters that make the sound /t/:

- In the simple past, **ed** makes the sound /t/ after:
  /p/ – stopp<u>ed</u>, /k/ – kick<u>ed</u>, /f/ – laugh<u>ed</u>, /d/– danc<u>ed</u>, /sh/ – wish<u>ed</u>, /ch/– watch<u>ed</u>

- **th** makes the sound /t/ in words like <u>th</u>yme, <u>Th</u>ailand and <u>Th</u>ompson

- In pizza, the first **z** sounds like /t/

/kikt/

Please note (if you are still awake), **t**'s sister sound **d** follows some of the same patterns as **t** (but it's not nearly as bad.)

- In the **final** position, /d/ sounds like a ½ d (*unreleased*), so **baa** and **bad** sound the same.
- /d/ disappears when followed by an **n**: gar<u>d</u>en becomes /gar'en/

Real Live English

When a word **ending** in **d** is in **front** of **you,** the sound is /ja/.

    Di<u>d you</u> = /**dija**/   Di<u>d you</u> get a haircut? = /**dija** get a haircut/

When a word **ending** in **d** is in **front** of **your** or **you're** the sound is /jer/.

    Di<u>d your</u> = /**dijer**/   Di<u>d your</u> sister get one? = /**dijer** sister get one/

It makes learners happy and excited when they can reconcile *classroom* English with the English they experience in the real world.

Hurray! Hurray!

Lesson Idea

This is a great time for a lesson on the simple past.
    ed = /d/, /t/ or /id/

This is even great for advanced students because it is grammar they already know but they have never sounded like native speakers before. I have never met a student who didn't want to sound like a native speaker. Sure, the grammar might be easy for them, but they never *lookt* at it this way before.

New information and a confidence builder as well!

Not-So-Simple Past

Make the verb in the simple past and put it in the category /d/, /t/ or /id/, depending on the sound the **ed** makes.

    play   talk   wait   shop   add   tie smile
    /d/   /t/   /id/
    played   talked   waited…

Past Tense Flashcards PDF (24 cards) available as a free download from **www.ThompsonLanguageCenter.com**

English Phonetic Alphabet   Student Page

More Practice

Use the English Phonetic Alphabet symbol to indicate the sound of the underlined letter in each of the words below. The first one is done for you.

Beginner

<u>b</u>oy	/ b /	<u>c</u>ap	/ /	A<u>s</u>ia	/ /
<u>d</u>og	/ /	<u>th</u>in	/ /	bei<u>g</u>e	/ /
<u>f</u>ive	/ /	<u>c</u>elery	/ /	<u>h</u>ome	/ /
<u>n</u>ever	/ /	<u>th</u>is	/ /	jui<u>c</u>e	/ /
<u>y</u>ellow	/ /	<u>g</u>iant	/ /	w<u>a</u>lk	/ /
<u>sh</u>ip	/ /	<u>ph</u>one	/ /	<u>z</u>ero	/ /
<u>ch</u>air	/ /	ri<u>ng</u>	/ /	pea<u>s</u>	/ /

Intermediate

<u>s</u>ugar	/ /	no<u>s</u>e	/ /	gara<u>g</u>e	/ /
oran<u>g</u>e	/ /	fa<u>c</u>e	/ /	E<u>n</u>glish	/ /
s<u>ch</u>ool	/ /	na<u>t</u>ion	/ /	o<u>c</u>ean	/ /
plea<u>s</u>e	/ /	fa<u>th</u>er	/ /	<u>h</u>our	/ /
<u>w</u>rite	/ /	<u>ph</u>oto	/ /	laugh<u>ed</u>	/ /
ne<u>ck</u>	/ /	<u>k</u>now	/ /	ca<u>l</u>m	/ /
mou<u>th</u>	/ /	de<u>b</u>t	/ /	dog<u>s</u>	/ /

Advanced

wa<u>t</u>er	/ /	to<u>ng</u>ue	/ /	autum<u>n</u>	/ /
clo<u>th</u>es	/ /	<u>c</u>ello	/ /	si<u>g</u>n	/ /
<u>r</u>hino	/ /	u<u>s</u>ual	/ /	dan<u>c</u>ed	/ /
pre<u>tt</u>y	/ /	We<u>d</u>nesday	/ /	na<u>t</u>ure	/ /
debri<u>s</u>	/ /	un<u>i</u>on	/ /	e<u>d</u>ucation	/ /
<u>wh</u>at	/ /	ques<u>t</u>ion	/ /	ans<u>w</u>er	/ /
<u>w</u>ho	/ /	ask<u>ed</u>	/ /	<u>Ch</u>ristian	/ /
thou<u>gh</u>	/ /	talk<u>ed</u>	/ /	bu<u>tt</u>er	/ /
bu<u>s</u>y	/ /	thum<u>b</u>	/ /	ve<u>h</u>icle	/ /
Bri<u>t</u>ish	/ /	pi<u>zz</u>a	/ /	<u>c</u>apital	/ /
plum<u>b</u>er	/ /	Feb<u>r</u>uary	/ /	lan<u>g</u>uage	/ /
of<u>t</u>en	/ /	wi<u>th</u>	/ /	<u>qu</u>arter	/ /
<u>i</u>sland	/ /	e<u>x</u>am	/ /	<u>qu</u>iche	/ /

www.thompsonlanguagecenter.com

Teacher Page   English Phonetic Alphabet

Student Transformation

Students become excited when they read the poem Ol' Frenz.

When the poem is read to them, their eyes follow the version on the right side of the page, where native speakers read from the left. For the first time, the students can *see* the *sounds* they *hear*. When they read a stanza of the poem aloud, they sound just like native English speakers, and it is thrilling for them.

The students can't wait for their turn to read the poem to the class. They grumble when break time comes and they have to stop. For individuals who were loath to open their mouths the week before, this is akin to a miracle. They leave the classroom peaceful, free and alive. Their transformation into confident English speakers has begun.

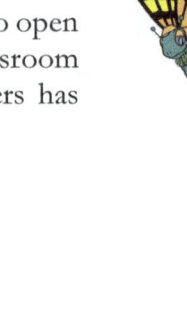

Answer Key

Beginner

boy /b/	cap /k/	Asia /zh/	dog /d/	thin /TH/	beige /zh/
five /f/	celery /s/	home /h/	never /n/	this /Th/	juice /s/
yellow /y/	giant /j/	walk /w/	ship /sh/	phone /f/	zero /z/
chair /Ch/	ring /Ng/	peas /z/			

Intermediate

sugar /sh/	nose /z/	garage /zh/	orange /j/	face /s/	English /Ng/
school /k/	nation /sh/	ocean /sh/	please /z/	father /Th/	hour /Ø/
write /Ø/	photo /f/	laughed /t/	neck /k/	know /Ø/	calm /Ø/
mouth /TH/	debt /Ø/	dogs /z/			

Advanced

water /d/	tongue /Ng/	autumn /Ø/	clothes /Ø/	cello /Ch/	sign /Ø/
rhino /Ø/	usual /zh/	danced /s/	pretty /d/	Wednesday /Ø/	nature /Ch/
debris /Ø/	union /y/	education /j/	what /Ø/	question /j/	answer /Ø/
who /Ø/	asked /t/	Christian /j/	though /Ø/	talked /t/	butter /d/
busy /z/	thumb /Ø/	vehicle /Ø/	British /d/	pizza /t/	capital /k/
plumber /Ø/	February /Ø/	language /w/	often /Ø/	with /TH/	quarter /kw/
island /Ø/	exam /gz/	quiche /k/			

© Judy Thompson 2009

English Phonetic Alphabet   Student Page

Putting it All Together

Read poems to practice *speaking*. This is the same poem printed twice.

On the left, it is in regular print.   On the right, the consonants have been replaced with EPA sound symbols.

Which side do you like better?

What the poem looks like: What the poem sounds like:

<u>Old Friends</u>   Ol' Frenz

We walked and talked,   we wakt an takt
And talked and walked.   an takt an wakt
Walked and talked,   wakt an takt
Talked and walked.   takt an wakt

We sat in a garden,   we sat in a garden
And looked at the flowers.   an lookt at the flowerz
We talked and talked,   we takt an takt
For hours and hours.   for ourz an ourz

He drank coffee,   he drank kofee
And I drank tea.   an I drank tea
We sat and talked,   we sat an takt
From one to three.   from one to three

We talked about him,   we takt about him
We talked about us.   we takt about us
Then we walked to the corner,   then we wakt to the korner
To get the bus.   to get the bus

We waited and waited,   we waided an waided
The bus was late.   the bus waz late
So we stood and talked,   so we stood an takt
From four to eight.   from for to Ayt

(Author Unknown)

Teacher Page   English Phonetic Alphabet

Silent Consonants

H is often *Silent* in Pronouns

	English looks like this:	**English sounds like this:**
he – 'e	What does **he** do for a living?	What does **'e** do for a living?
his – 'is	What's **his** name?	What's **'is** name?
him – 'im	Have **him** call me.	Have **'im** call me.
her – 'er	Take **her** out for dinner.	Take **'er** out for dinner.
them – 'em	Give **them** hell.	Give **'em** hell.

There is a fabulous little book with a tape called *Whaddaya Say* by Nina Weinstein, full of dandy exercises comparing **written** English (which Nina calls CAREFUL (SLOW) PRONUNCIATION) and *spoken* English (which Nina refers to as RELAXED (FAST) PRONUNCIATION) – a *must have* for every classroom.

I'm Learning How to Spell
(Author Unknown)

I'm learning how to spell today;
I'm doing very well,
I know that **ex**it starts with **x**,
And **el**ephant with **l**.

There's **k** for **c**ape and **c**ane and **c**ake
And **q** is for **cu**cumber,
Forest starts with **4**. I think…
No – **4** is just a number.

Birth**day** ends with the letter **a**
And ea**sy** ends with **z**.
o comes last in scarecr**ow**,
And bab**y** ends with **e**.

It gets harder, I suppose,
As you go along,
But spelling seems quite simple now.
Perhaps I could be **rong**.

★Double consonants are pronounced once.
- ba**ll** is pronounced /bal/
- pe**pp**er is pronounced /pe per/
- ca**rr**ot is pronounced /ka rot/

Exceptions

Double **c** – both **c**s are pronounced separately as /ks/ in a**cc**ept, a**cc**ess…

In North America, double **t**s sound like /d/ – pre**tt**y, bu**tt**er

Because **English is crazy**.

© Judy Thompson 2009

English Phonetic Alphabet   Student Page

Silent Consonants

Beware of **Silent Consonants** – they are everywhere!

Silent consonants are letters that represent no sound.

Ø is the symbol when a letter is silent.

li<u>gh</u>t   <u>w</u>rite

i<u>s</u>land   autum<u>n</u>

si<u>g</u>n   s<u>c</u>ience

wa<u>l</u>k   plum<u>b</u>er

ans<u>w</u>er   <u>k</u>nee

Double Consonants

Double consonants are pronounced **once**: ca<u>rr</u>ot – one **r** disappears.

ca<u>rr</u>ot   ha<u>mm</u>er

/ka_ rot/   /ha_ mer/

Exceptions: In English, there are always exceptions. Peek over at the teacher's page on the left. ⇐

www.thompsonlanguagecenter.com   49

Vowels

As crazy as the consonants are – the vowels are worse. Vowels are so irregular, the computer generation doesn't always bother with them. Now there is **txtng**.

A: **so wut r u up2 tday** So what are you up to today?
B: **nt much** Not much.
A: **cya dood ttyl tho** See you dude. Talk to you later though.
B: **lol fo sho** /Laugh out loud/ (ha ha) for sure.

Vowel Sounds

A consonant is a stopped or restricted sound; a vowel is an elastic or unrestricted sound. [Hook a rubber band between your thumbs, pull your hands apart] and say, Ooooooooooh, aaaaaaaaaah, eeeeeeeeeyk! These are vowels.

A vowel sound is an elastic sound. It s t r e t c h e s.

There are **16** vowel sounds in English, represented by **5** familiar alphabet symbols (a, e, i, o, u) and **11** new EPA symbols. Spelling vowel sounds is nothing short of ridiculous – anything goes. Any vowel or combination of vowels can spell any vowel sound at any time. For example, there are at least **14** different spellings for the vowel sound in bl<u>ue</u>; n<u>ew</u>, y<u>ou</u>, tw<u>o</u>, m<u>oo</u>, v<u>iew</u>, cl<u>ue</u>, wh<u>o</u>, d<u>o</u>, sh<u>oe</u>, thr<u>ough</u>, fl<u>u</u>, j<u>ui</u>ce, b<u>eau</u>tiful, S<u>iou</u>x, S<u>au</u>lt, and so on. There are no rules.

It sounds depressing, doesn't it? Well, don't be discouraged – help is on the way. Once students have heard enough *spoken* English (about 300 hours), the sounds of words begin to be stored away mentally. With their personal warehouse of vocabulary and some speaking training, ESL students begin to override the confusing visual cues of the alphabet and spelling in *written* English and learn to speak English from the sound of it. This process more closely mimics first-language acquisition.

Even though vowels can be a nightmare, it's important to be able to hear and recreate them individually. A fast and simple system for learning English vowel sounds is with the Thompson Vowel System found on page 55. One of the first things learned in any new language is the words for different colors. Fortunately, each color word in English holds a different vowel sound. It's not difficult to learn the vowel sounds contained in each color. Connecting the sounds to colors establishes a solid bridge between English vowel sounds and undecipherable English vowel spellings.

It can't be said enough – **words don't sound like they look**, and learners *have to* LISTEN to hundreds of hours of English before they can speak it.

English Phonetic Alphabet   Student Page

Vowel Sounds

Vowel sounds are *elastic* sounds.

AAAAaaaaaaay   EEEEeeeeeeeey

They *s t r e t c h*.

There are **five** vowels in the Roman alphabet – A, E, I, O, U.

But there are **16** vowel sounds in English! Spelling vowel sounds is **hard**, because spelling doesn't make sense – like consonants, only worse.

There are **14** /Ay/ sounds in this short postcard spelled **7** different ways.

Gray Vacation

It rained for eight days straight. But it was OK. Every day we stayed in the café and ate great soufflé.

Gr<u>ay</u>, v<u>a</u>cation, r<u>ai</u>n, <u>ei</u>ght, d<u>ay</u>, str<u>ai</u>ght, <u>k</u>, d<u>ay</u>, st<u>ay</u>ed caf<u>e</u> <u>a</u>te gr<u>ea</u>t souttl<u>e</u>
  ay a   ai ei   e   ea   é

This is a but a small sample of the craziness of vowels. **Vowel sounds can be spelled many different ways** and **every vowel symbol can represent many different sounds**.[5]

- Vowel Sounds can be spelled many different ways
- Every vowel letter can represent many different sounds
- *Long vowels* are long because they have *two* sounds
- *Short vowels* are short because they have only *one* sound
- The letter names A, E, I, O, U are all long vowels

---

[5] See Appendix 4.

Don't Lie to Your Students

Whoever said, When two vowels go a-walking, the first one does the talking was whacked. Don't tell students things that aren't true. English is confusing enough.

When two vowels go a-walking,
the first one does the talking.

 Which vowel is talking in Have a p<u>ie</u>ce of p<u>ie</u>, my fr<u>ie</u>nd?

Let's look at **ea** – <u>ea</u>r, h<u>ea</u>d, p<u>ea</u>r, gr<u>ea</u>t, h<u>ea</u>rt, <u>ea</u>rth, S<u>ea</u>n, r<u>ea</u>ct, cr<u>ea</u>te, acr<u>ea</u>ge…

When **e** and **a** go a-walking, they make any sound they want! So this is NOT A RULE!

i before e except after c
or when it says ay
as in n<u>ei</u>ghbor and w<u>ei</u>gh

This rule fails to apply to height, heifer, forfeit, Sheila, Keith, Leigh, seize, inveigle, caffeine, protein, codeine, either, neither, geisha, sheik(h), leisure, seizure – which actually means this is also NOT A RULE!

Who makes this stuff up and tells it to students?

They ought to be arrested.

Students believe **everything** teachers say, so be really honest with them.

There are No Rules

The vowel pair **ea** makes **six** different sounds in this short note.

Take Heart

To create peace on Earth,

break bread with your dearest friends.

h<u>ea</u>rt, cr<u>ea</u>te, p<u>ea</u>ce, <u>Ea</u>rth, br<u>ea</u>k, br<u>ea</u>d, d<u>ea</u>rest
 Ar   EyAy   Ey   Er   Ay   e   Ey

There are **no rules**, so don't let anyone tell you any *rules*. But…

Don't worry!

There is an **easy** answer, and here it is.

Painting? No, not painting.

Colors are the answer! There are **16** vowel sounds in **16** colors in English. Learn the *colors,* and you learn the sounds.

For example, the vowel sound /Ay/ is in **gray,** as in *gray day.*

Spelling doesn't matter. d<u>ay</u>, r<u>ai</u>n, <u>ei</u>ght, <u>a</u>te, gr<u>ea</u>t, K, caf<u>é</u>… are all **gray**.

In **red** is the sound /e/.   h<u>ea</u>d, s<u>ai</u>d, g<u>ue</u>ss, m<u>a</u>ny, fr<u>ie</u>nd… are all **red**.

As in *red head*

Never mind the spelling. Listen for the **color** of the word.

The *POWER* of the Thompson Vowel Chart

Students have to not only hear but use a word like **women** with crazy spelling 50 to 70 times before they can master it and say the /i/ sound for the **o** letter. And that is only one common word! With the **Thompson Vowel Chart,** the student learns that **women** is PINK. They learn very quickly to take the vowel sound from the cue color and correctly pronounce /wimen/ the first time and forever after. It takes an intermediate student less than an hour to master the color chart connection. It takes a novice student longer. The benefits stay with them long after they have left the classroom.

For students, the alphabet system doesn't work, and they scramble for ways to process and remember the pronunciation of words accurately. With the Thompson Vowel Chart, the teacher doesn't need to pronounce the word at all. The student sees a word like **build** or **busy** and the teacher says It's PINK. The student will confidently pronounce the words correctly – /bild/, /bizEy/ – without necessarily having heard the words. It's magic! Students who learn the **Thompson Vowel System** swear by it.

The **Vowel Chart** is the most important piece of paper a student will ever get in school. If their house is on fire, they are to run in and get this piece of paper!

Makes for odd conversations, though.

What color is **grass**?

BLACK!

Instructional Videos

YouTube – on the *Thompson Language Center* channel click **Judy Thompson Teaching Speaking   VIEW FULL PLAYLIST** for 18 short videos that take you through the entire *English is Crazy* program.

Poster PDFs
A variety of colorful 2'x3' classroom posters on display at
www.ThompsonLanguageCenter.com
Order any of the printable PDFs for $5.00 US @ by email from
judy@thompsonlanguagecenter.com

Flashcard Word List PDFs
The flashcard lists featured in the YouTube videos above are **FREE DOWNLOADS**
24 Past Tense 'ed' (video #4), 16 Vowel Color Cards (video #9) 200

English Phonetic Alphabet   Student Page

Thompson Vowel Chart©

Color Word	Color	EPA	Phonetic Spelling	Example	Phonetic with 'f'
gray		/Ay/	/grAy/	made	face
black		/a/	/blak/	mad	fat
green		/Ey/	/grEyn/	Pete	feel
red		/e/	/red/	pet	fell
white		/Iy/	/wIyt/	bite	file
pink		/i/	/piNgk/	bit	fill
gold		/ow/	/gowld/	note	fold
olive		/o/	/oliv/	not	fall
blue		/Uw/	/blUw/	cute	food
mustard		/u/	/mustErd/	cut	fun
wood		/^/	/w^d/	good	full
turquoise		/Oy/	/tErkOyz/	boy	foil
brown		/Aw/	/brAwn/	cow	found
purple		/Er/	/pErpul/	girl	first
charcoal		/Ar/	/chArkOwl/	car	far
orange		/Or/	/Orenj/	door	four

© Judy Thompson, 2001

Q: What color is?

cat   hat   mask   apple   laugh   plaid

A: ■ **black.** They are all black – /k**a**t/, /h**a**t/, /m**a**sk/, /**a**pel/, /gr**a**s/, /l**a**f/, /pl**a**d/

As in *black cat*

www.thompsonlanguagecenter.com   55

Teacher Page English Phonetic Alphabet

Lesson Idea

Flash Cards[6]

Hold up simple ordinary flash cards with simple ordinary words on them and say…

What color is | tree | Somebody in the class will say, Green.

Start with the order they have been presented to the students on the first day. Give them a chance to upload a *sound* reference system in their brains using the **Vowel Color Chart**. It is amazing how quickly they do this.

Gray and black take the longest to process. They are the first colors in the system, and reprogramming takes a few minutes.

| rain | is gray, so are | train | | name | | face | | eight |

Be patient; let learners figure it out. Students really appreciate this system. It is a gift they will use for the rest of their lives.

For a beginner class, a super teacher could color-code flash cards:

go   boat   know   sew   toe

Some students have an understanding of **long** and **short** vowels. This is how they fit in:

l o n g   short

ā   /Ay/ - gray   ă   /a/ - black
ē   /Ey/ - green   ĕ   /e/ - red
ī   /Iy/ - white   ĭ   /i/ - pink
ō   /Ow/ - yell<u>ow</u>   ŏ   /o/ - olive
ū   /Uw/ - blue   ŭ   /u/ - mustard

Long vowels are l – o – n – g; they each have **two letters**. They take twice as long to say as **short vowels** – which are only **one letter**.

---

[6] Make your own flashcards from the **Flashcard Word List** available as a free download from www.ThompsonLanguageCenter.com

© Judy Thompson 2009

English Phonetic Alphabet   Student Page

Easy Vowels

black /a/ **is** an **easy** vowel. Here are some more.

ESL students have no trouble hearing or saying these vowel sounds using color – *tree* is **green** /Ey/; so is *seat* and *people*.

Spelling is crazy. Read the **words out loud** and **listen for the** *color*.

/Ay/	/Ey/	/e/	/ow/	/Ar/	/Or/
gray	green	red	old	dark	orange
day	tree	head	gold	charcoal	orange
play	me	said	go	car	or
rain	seat	get	toe	star	door
eight	people	guess	note	are	for
made	piece	friend	know	R	four
great	teeth	many	boat	park	pour
hey	receipt	S	beau	market	war
K	Judy	ready	sew	heart	store
café	ski	exit	though	farm	court
buffet	3	very	ghost	garlic	4

Easy Beginner Vowel Quiz

What **color** are the following words: Hint: Read the words out loud.

name / /	no / /	heart / /
paint / /	snow / /	store / /
tree / /	road / /	floor / /
ski / /	gold / /	three / /
bed / /	card / /	great / /
guest / /	start / /	goat / /

www.thompsonlanguagecenter.com   57

Teacher Page   English Phonetic Alphabet

English is Crazy! How did You Learn it?

Read aloud to students. Everyone likes to be read to. Children's books help students reconcile that words don't sound like they look. They also stockpile the sounds of words.

The Cat in the Hat I sat there with Sally.
by Dr. Seuss: We sat there, we *two*.
And I said, "How I wish
We had something to *do*!

Adult students are in such a hurry to learn English right away that they want to run before they can crawl. Support the learning process from the beginning. Read to them. Have them **listen** to simple English stories.

Developmental psychologists identify that *crawling* is an essential stage in learning to *walk*. Language crawling is **listening** to children's books. Keep books with *Little Red Riding Hood, Jack and the Beanstock, Mother Goose, Nursery Rhymes* and *Aesop's Fables* in your classroom. They are an indispensable part of the *speaking* process.

Answer Key

Easy Beginner Vowel Quiz

n<u>a</u>me	/ʌy/	n<u>o</u>	/Ow/	h<u>ear</u>t	/ʌr/
p<u>ai</u>nt	/ʌy/	sn<u>ow</u>	/Ow/	st<u>o</u>re	/Or/
tr<u>ee</u>	/Ey/	r<u>oa</u>d	/Ow/	fl<u>oo</u>r	/Or/
sk<u>i</u>	/Ey/	g<u>o</u>ld	/Ow/	thr<u>ee</u>	/Ey/
b<u>e</u>d	/e/	c<u>ar</u>d	/ʌr/	gr<u>ea</u>t	/ʌy/
g<u>ue</u>st	/e/	st<u>ar</u>t	/ʌr/	g<u>oa</u>t	/Ow/

© Judy Thompson 2009

English Phonetic Alphabet   Student Page

Not-So-Easy Vowels

ESL students have to *slow down* and say words *carefully* to hear these vowel sounds.

/Iy/ wh**i**te kn**i**ght	/i/ p**i**nk flam**i**ngo	/uw/ bl**ue** sh**oe**	/^/ g**oo**d w**oo**d	/oy/ turqu**oi**se t**oy**s	/aw/ br**ow**n c**ow**
b**i**te	**i**t	d**o**	p**u**t	b**oy**	**ow**n
h**ei**ght	**i**s	y**ou**	b**oo**k	n**oi**se	v**ow**el
I, **eye**, **aye**	w**i**th	wh**o**	l**oo**k	**oi**l	s**ou**nd
p**ie**	pr**e**tty	n**ew**	h**oo**k	l**oy**al	h**ou**se
b**uy**, b**ye**	b**u**sy	b**oo**t	w**ou**ld	r**oy**al	c**ou**ch
g**ui**de	b**ui**ld	gl**ue**	c**ou**ld	l**aw**yer	h**ou**r
sk**y**	m**y**th	c**u**te	st**oo**d	Ill**i**n**oi**s	pl**ough**
aisle	w**o**men	j**ui**ce	sh**ou**ld		
5, **9**	**6**	b**eau**tiful	w**o**man		
		2			

Intermediate Vowel Quiz

This quiz contains all the vowel sounds up to now including **gray /Ay/**, **black /a/**, **red /e/** from the introduction and all the easy vowels **green /Ey/**, **white /Iy/**, **pink /i/**, **yellow /Ow/**, **charcoal /Ar/**, **orange /Or/** and the not-so-easy vowels from this page.

day	/Ay/	why	/ /	door	/ /
train	/ /	sigh	/ /	you	/ /
cat	/ /	is	/ /	food	/ /
back	/ /	women	/ /	juice	/ /
three	/ /	slow	/ /	book	/ /
each	/ /	dough	/ /	could	/ /
bed	/ /	rose	/ /	boy	/ /
guess	/ /	art	/ /	voice	/ /
friend	/ /	mark	/ /	brown	/ /
pie	/ /	more	/ /	mouse	/ /

www.thompsonlanguagecenter.com

Teacher Page English Phonetic Alphabet

Teacher Talk

Lesson Idea

The **number one** problem vowel for students to hear and recreate is /o/ as in **not** – color name **OLIVE**. Students try to say it with their mouths shut. No matter what their first language is, hot coffee sounds like hut cuffee. To get them to make the sound, remind them of a trip to the doctor where the doctor always says:

Open your mouth and say "AAAhhhhh!"

This is the sound we are looking for. If their mouths aren't wide open, they aren't doing it. (They are probably self-conscious about opening their mouths so wide.) /o/ is everywhere – father, office, off, on, dog, walk, talk, shop, hospital, cough, caught, got, clock, all, wall, doctor, possible, closet… As the vocabulary comes up, make a **BIG CLASS** /o/ **LIST** on the wall – they will refer to it over and over again.

If they still call this hut cuffee after the lesson, I pretend I don't know what they are saying – Pardon, me? What? I don't know what you want. They laugh☺ and correct themselves. It's all in good fun.

MUSTARD and **PURPLE** get the same treatment. Olive, mustard and purple account for the majority of letter pronunciation troubles.

Intermediate Vowel Quiz Answers

day	/Ay/	why	/Iy/	door	/Or/
train	/Ay/	sigh	/Iy/	you	/Uw/
cat	/a/	is	/i/	food	/Uw/
back	/a/	women	/i/	juice	/Uw/
three	/Ey/	slow	/Ow/	book	/^/
each	/Ey/	dough	/Ow/	could	/^/
bed	/e/	rose	/Ow/	boy	/Oy/
guess	/e/	art	/Ar/	voice	/Oy/
friend	/e/	mark	/Ar/	brown	/Aw/
pie	/Iy/	more	/Or/	mouse	/Aw/

© Judy Thompson 2009

English Phonetic Alphabet　　　　　　Student Page

Hard Vowels

ESL students have problems with short vowel sounds, especially:

olive /o/, mustard /u/, and purple /Er/

/o/	/u/	/Er/
olive	**mustard**	**purple**
olive	**custard**	**nurple***
h**o**t	**u**p	h**er**
c**o**ffee	b**u**s	w**ere**
f**a**ther	**u**nder	g**ir**l
br**oa**d	m**o**ther	n**ur**se
c**ou**gh	c**ou**sin	w**or**d
awe	fl**oo**d	**ear**th
l**aw**	th**e**	f**ur**
	w**a**s	y**our**
	d**oe**s	s**u**gar
	bec**au**se	c**o**lonel
	one	

*nurple: I made it up. You can do that with English. It's fun!

Advanced Vowel Quiz

c**o**ffee / /	w**or**k / /	n**i**ght / /
f**a**ther / /	p**ur**se / /	w**o**men / /
office / /	c**e**rtain / /	n**o**se / /
c**au**ght / /	c**ur**tain / /	sch**oo**l / /
c**ou**sin / /	tr**ee** / /	b**u**tter / /
uncle / /	tr**ai**n / /	t**ow**n / /
br**o**ther / /	b**a**t / /	l**aw**yer / /
once / /	b**e**st / /	f**our** / /

www.thompsonlanguagecenter.com　　　　61

Teacher Page		English Phonetic Alphabet

Lesson Ideas

What color is your name?
"Judy" -   Ju   dy
         /ʊw/ /ɛy/   I am blue / green.

ABC/123

What color are the letters of the alphabet? Simple materials students are familiar with work well because they have never looked at them this way before – from a sound perspective. Advanced students look down their noses at the alphabet and say *this is too easy*… but they can't do it.☺ They stumble because they are not as smart with the sound alphabet as they think. Start with basics.

A is gray /ʌy/	F red	K gray	P green	U blue	Z green/red
B is green /ɛy/	G green	L red	Q blue	V green	1 mustard
C green	H gray	M red	R charcoal	W mustard	2 blue
D green	I white	N red	S red	X red	3 green
E green	J gray	O yellow	T green	Y white	4 orange

A /ʌy/	F /ef/	K /kʌy/	P /pɛy/	U /yʊw/	Z /zɛy/ USA or /zed/ Canada
B /bɛy/	G /jɛy/	L /el/	Q /kyʊw/	V /vɛy/	1 /wun/
C /sɛy/	H /ʌych/	M /em/	R /ʌr/	W /dubel yʊw/	2 /tʊw/
D /dɛy/	I /ɪy/	N /en/	S /es/	X /eks/	3 /THrɛy/
E /ɛy/	J /jʌy/	O /ow/	T /tɛy/	Y /wɪy/	4 /fɔr/

Be patient. The 40 sounds of English are the foundation of *speaking*.

Time spent in class on these *listening* and *speaking* basics will pay off one hundred fold.

It's easy to make it fun.

Advanced Vowel Quiz Answers

c**o**ffee	/o/	w**o**rk	/ɛr/	n**igh**t	/ɪy/
f**a**ther	/o/	p**ur**se	/ɛr/	w**o**men	/i/
office	/o/	c**er**tain	/ɛr/	n**o**se	/ow/
c**au**ght	/o/	c**ur**tain	/ɛr/	sch**oo**l	/ʊw/
c**ou**sin	/u/	tr**ee**	/ɛy/	b**u**tter	/u/
uncle	/u/	tr**ai**n	/ʌy/	t**ow**n	/ʌw/
br**o**ther	/u/	b**a**t	/a/	l**aw**yer	/ɔy/
once	/u/	b**e**st	/e/	f**ou**r	/ɔr/

© Judy Thompson 2009

Letters   Student Page

Vowel Hunt

There are **16** vowel sounds in English and **16** English Phonetic Alphabet (EPA) vowel symbols. Some symbols are used more than once in this exercise. Print the EPA sound symbol for the underlined letters in the slash brackets beside each word. The first one is done for you.

Hint: Read the words out loud.

Per<u>u</u>   /uw/

Th<u>ai</u>land   / /

Sp<u>ai</u>n   / /

<u>Au</u>stria   / /

S<u>ou</u>th Africa   / /

Sw<u>e</u>den   / /

Ch<u>i</u>na   / /

R<u>u</u>ssia   / /

H<u>u</u>ngary   / /

Mexic<u>o</u>   / /

V<u>i</u>etnam   / /

Kor<u>e</u>a   / /

P<u>a</u>kistan   / /

Denm<u>a</u>rk   / /

Ur<u>u</u>guay   / /

V<u>e</u>nezuela   / /

The Ph<u>i</u>lippines   / /

Z<u>a</u>mbia   / /

G<u>e</u>rmany   / /

Mal<u>a</u>ysia   / /

T<u>u</u>rkey   / /

N<u>o</u>rway   / /

W<u>a</u>les   / /

<u>E</u>ngland   / /

www.thompsonlanguagecenter.com

Teacher Page   Letters

Play on Words

The silly business of **letters ≠ sounds** in English makes for a lot of fun.

*How do you pronounce **ghoti**?*

gh = /f/ as in cou<u>gh</u>
 o = /i/ as in w<u>o</u>men
 ti = /sh/ as in na<u>ti</u>on

*The word is pronounced **fish**.*   G.B. Shaw

In ***You Don't Say!***, Alfred Holt (1937) offers this amusing bit of verse.

Some greet with lusty 'Rah's

A reference to vase.

Another bares his claws

At folks who don't say vase.

But many use the phrase,

"Please put these in a vase,"

While still a stronger case

We now can make a vase.

Answer Key

Pe<u>r</u>u	/Uw/	P<u>a</u>kistan	/a/
Th<u>ai</u>land	/Iy/	Denm<u>a</u>rk	/Ar/
Sp<u>ai</u>n	/Ay/	U<u>r</u>uguay	/u/
<u>Au</u>stria	/o/	V<u>e</u>nezuela	/e/
S<u>ou</u>th Africa	/Aw/	The Ph<u>i</u>lippines	/i/
Sw<u>e</u>den	/Ey/	Z<u>a</u>mbia	/a/
Ch<u>i</u>na	/Iy/	Ge<u>r</u>many	/Er/
R<u>u</u>ssia	/u/	Mal<u>a</u>ysia	/Ay/
H<u>u</u>ngary	/u/	T<u>u</u>rkey	/Er/
Mexi<u>c</u>o	/Ow/	N<u>o</u>rway	/Or/
V<u>ie</u>tnam	/Ey/	W<u>a</u>les	/Ay/
Ko<u>r</u>ea	/Ey/	<u>E</u>ngland	/i/

© Judy Thompson 2009

Letters   Student Page

The English Phonetic Alphabet

24 Consonants
/b/, /d/, /f/, /g/, /h/, /j/, /k/, /l/, /m/, /n/, /p/, /r/, /s/, /t/, /v/, /w/, /y/, /z/
/Ch/, /Sh/, /TH/, /Th/, /Ng/, /Zh/

16 Vowels
/Ay/, /a/, /Ey/, /e/, /Iy/, /i/, /Ow/, /o/, /Uw/, /u/, /^/, /Oy/, /Aw/, /Er/, /Ar/, /Or/

Old Friends

Here is *Old Friends* from page 47. On the right, the consonants **and the vowels** have been replaced with EPA, the sound symbols.

What the poem looks like: **What the poem sounds like:**

Old Friends   **Owld frenz**

We walked and talked,   wEy wokt an tokt
And talked and walked.   an tokt an wokt
Walked and talked,   wokt an tokt
Talked and walked.   tokt an wokt

We sat in a garden,   wEy sat in a gar'n
And looked at the flowers.   an l^kt at the flAwErz
We talked and talked,   wEy tokt an tokt
For hours and hours.   for Awrz an Awrz

He drank coffee,   hEy drank kofEy
And I drank tea.   an Iy drank tEy
We sat and talked,   wEy sat an tokt
From one to three.   from wun to THrEy

We talked about him,   wEy tokt abAwt him
We talked about us.   wEy tokt abAwt us
Then we walked to the corner,   then wEy wokt to the kOrnEr
To get the bus.   to get the bus

We waited and waited,   wEy wAydid an wAydid
The bus was late.   the bus wuz lAyt
So we stood and talked,   so wEy st^d an tokt
From four to eight.   frum fOr to Ayt

(Author Unknown)

www.thompsonlanguagecenter.com

Teacher Page　　　　　　　　　Letters

Long Vowel Rule of Thumb

Here is an 80% rule for **l o n g v o w e l s**:

The **e** on the end makes the vowel say its name.

An **e** at the end of a word is not pronounced, but it affects the sound of the vowel before it. Final **e** often (but not always) indicates the vowel has a long sound.

For example:　n<u>a</u>me (there is an **e** on the end) – the vowel **a** makes the sound /Ay/

　　　　　　　　t<u>i</u>me (there is an **e** on the end) – the vowel **i** makes the sound /Iy/

Look at a few examples:

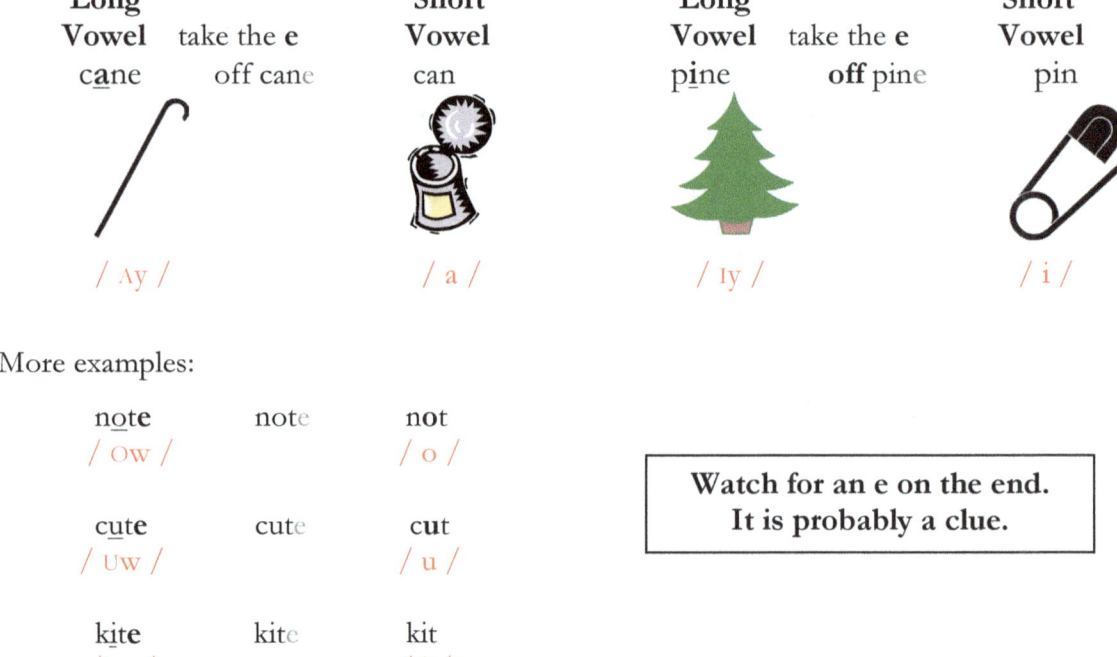

Long Vowel	take the e	Short Vowel		Long Vowel	take the e	Short Vowel
c<u>a</u>ne	off cane	can		p<u>i</u>ne	**off** pine	pin
/ Ay /		/ a /		/ Iy /		/ i /

More examples:

　　　n<u>o</u>te　　note　　not
　　　/ Ow /　　　　　　/ o /

　　　c<u>u</u>te　　cute　　cut
　　　/ Uw /　　　　　　/ u /

　　　k<u>i</u>te　　kite　　kit
　　　/ Iy /　　　　　　/ i /

> **Watch for an e on the end.
> It is probably a clue.**

Th<u>e</u>se are all over the **place** – m<u>a</u>ke, d<u>a</u>te, m<u>i</u>ne, h<u>o</u>me, wh<u>i</u>te, f<u>i</u>ve, h<u>o</u>pe, st<u>a</u>te, n<u>i</u>ne…

Exceptions:

　　　　　This is an **80% rule**. There are exceptions – this is English, after all.
　　　　　Home follows the rule, but it doesn't rhyme with **come** or **some**.
　　　　　Cove follows the rule, but it doesn't rhyme with **love** or **move**.
　　　　　Safe follows the rule, but it doesn't rhyme with **café**.

If you think it will **confuse** your class, don't tell them – play it by ear. If it's a class that really, really wants **rules** – **give** this one to them.

An **e** on the end may make the vowel say its name.

© Judy Thompson 2009　　　　　　　66

Just for Fun

Beginner

Circle the groups of words that rhyme.
(There are 6 circles in this exercise.) Hint: read the words out loud.

(new, blue, shoe) /uw/	white night light	do go to
wood good could	come home some	me three sea
put but cut	think pink sink	cake bake take

Bonus points – what is the color of each circle?

More Vowel Fun

Intermediate

Circle the groups of words that rhyme.
(There are seven circles in this exercise.)   Hint: read the words out loud.

noise boys toys	heart start part	their they're there
down town brown	food hood flood	red head said
love dove move	sunny money funny	four more door

Bonus points – what is the color of each circle?

www.thompsonlanguagecenter.com

Teacher Page   Letters

Beginner Answer Key

Beginner

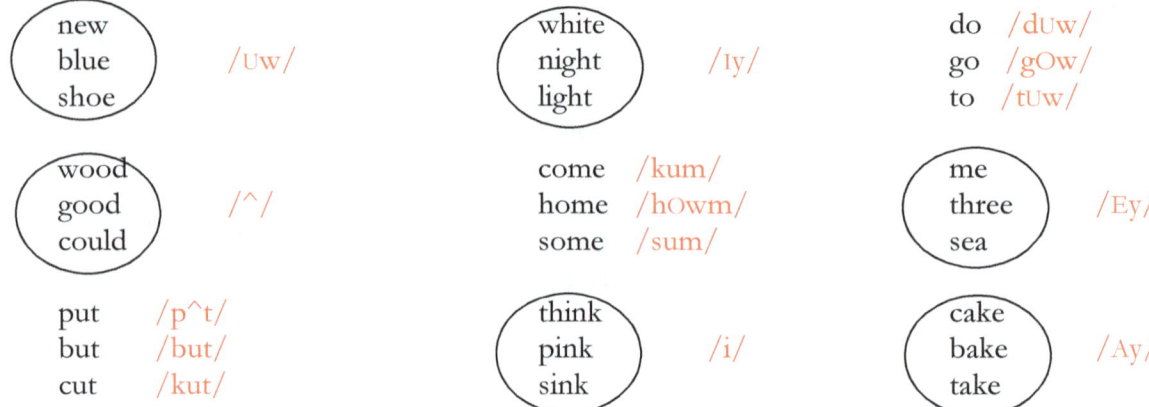

(new / blue / shoe)   /ʊw/

(wood / good / could)   /^/

put   /pʌt/
but   /bʌt/
cut   /kʌt/

(white / night / light)   /ɪy/

come   /kum/
home   /howm/
some   /sum/

(think / pink / sink)   /i/

do   /dʊw/
go   /gow/
to   /tʊw/

(me / three / sea)   /Ey/

(cake / bake / take)   /Ay/

Intermediate Answer Key

Intermediate

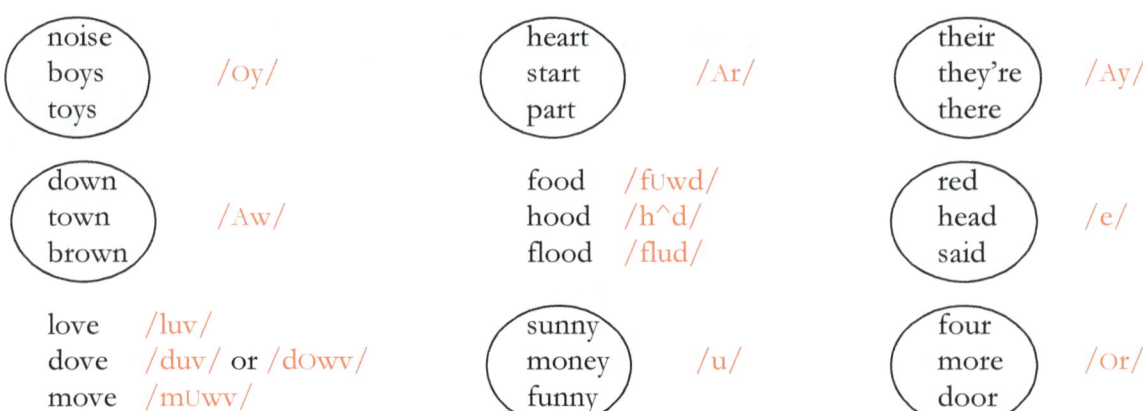

(noise / boys / toys)   /Oy/

(down / town / brown)   /Aw/

love   /luv/
dove   /duv/ or /dowv/
move   /mʊwv/

(heart / start / part)   /Ar/

food   /fʊwd/
hood   /h^d/
flood   /flud/

(sunny / money / funny)   /u/

(their / they're / there)   /Ay/

(red / head / said)   /e/

(four / more / door)   /Or/

 Bonus points – what is the color of each circle?

© Judy Thompson 2009   68

Letters   Student Page

Even More Vowel Fun!

Advanced

Circle the groups of words that rhyme.
(There are 14 circles in this exercise.)

bird	loose	these
word	juice	knees
heard	deuce	freeze

mouth	shows	thumb
both	nose	come
oath	froze	from

suit	eyes	love
boot	size	drove
route	pies	prove

twos	pie	how
news	sigh	now
fuse	why	throw

water	shoe	one
daughter	knew	fun
hotter	glue	son

laugh	eight	to
calf	great	do
staff	date	go

 Bonus points – what is the color of each circle?

Congratulations!

www.thompsonlanguagecenter.com   69

Teacher Page Letters

Advanced Answer Key

(bird word heard)	/ɛr/	(loose juice deuce)	/uw/	(these knees freeze)	/ɛy/
mouth /mʌwTH/ both /bowTH/ oath /owTH/		(shows nose froze)	/ow/	(thumb come from)	/u/
(suit boot route)	/uw/	(eyes size pies)	/ɪy/	love /luv/ drove drowv/ prove pruwv/	
(twos news fuse)	/uw/	(pie sigh why)	/ɪy/	how /hʌw/ now /nʌw/ throw /THrow/	
(water daughter hotter)	/o/	(shoe knew glue)	/uw/	(one fun son)	/u/
(laugh calf staff)	/a/	(eight great date)	/ʌy/	to /tuw/ do /duw/ go /gow/	

Transcriptions

Students love this. It's a game, and they attack *Transcriptions* as a Sudoku addict attacks a Sudoku puzzle. They race to see who can figure out the word the fastest. There's nothing like a game to make students forget they can't speak English. The quiet competitive students who have never before spoken in class start shouting out answers! ☺

© Judy Thompson 2009

Letters   Student Page

Transcriptions

Transcribe the following words from *spoken* English to *written* English.

Beginner

/grAy/ – gray	/mustErd/	/tUw/
/blak/	/w^d/	/THrEy/
/grEyn/	/tErkOyz/	/fOr/
/wIyt/	/brAwn/	/fIyv/
/piNgk/	/pErpel/	/siks/
/yelOw/	/ChArkOwl/	/Ayt/
/oliv/	/Orenj/	/nIyn/
/blUw/	/wun/	/twenEy/

Intermediate

/skUwl/	/Eyr/	/bOwt/
/klok/	/f^t/	/EyrAysEr/
/fAys/	/tUwTH/	/hArt/
/Iyz/	/THum/	/iz/
/bak/	/nEy/	/hiz/
/nek/	/bEyrd/	/wEy/
/nOwz/	/tEyChEr/	/ThAy/
/mAwTH/	/pAypEr/	/ShugEr/

Advanced

/wErd/	/bizEy/	/yUwnyun/
/hErd/	/laf/	/plEyz/
/bErd/	/uv/	/pEyz/
/wEr/	/kwEyn/	/pEys/
/wuns/	/kwik/	/sidEy/
/wimen/	/fOwn/	/ges/
/w^men/	/unyun/	/skwAyr/

Teacher Page   Letters

Invisible Consonants

They are *everywhere*.

Invisible consonants are **not printed,** but they are *spoken*.

Invisible consonants are the **opposite** of *silent* consonants.
Silent consonants are **printed** but make *no sound*.
Invisible consonants *make sound* but are **not printed**.

Vowel sounds cannot be pronounced together, so consonant sounds are inserted in predictable places – but they are not printed. Unlike good children, they are heard but not seen.

Transcriptions

Beginner

/grAy/ gray/grey	/mustErd/ mustard	/tUw/ two/to/too
/blak/ black	/w^d/ wood/would	/THrEy/ three
/grEyn/ green	/tErkOyz/ turquoise	/fOr/ four/for/fore
/wIyt/ white	/brAwn/ brown	/fIyv/ five
/piNgk/ pink	/pErpel/ purple	/siks/ six
/yelOw/ yellow	/ChArkOwl/ charcoal	/Ayt/ eight/ate
/oliv/ olive	/Orenj/ orange	/nIyn/ nine
/blUw/ blue	/wun/ one/won	/twenEy/ twenty

Intermediate

/skUwl/ school	/Eyr/ ear	/bOwt/ boat
/klok/ clock	/f^t/ foot	/EyrAysEr/ eraser
/fAys/ face	/tUwTH/ tooth	/hArt/ heart
/Iyz/ eyes	/THum/ thumb	/iz/ is
/bak/ back	/nEy/ knee	/hiz/ his
/nek/ neck	/bEyrd/ beard	/wEy/ we
/nOwz/ nose	/tEyChEr/ teacher	/thAy/ they
/mAwTH/ mouth	/pAypEr/ paper	/ShugEr/ suger

Advanced

/wErd/ word	/bizEy/ busy	/yUwnyun/ union
/hErd/ heard/herd	/laf/ laugh	/plEyz/ please
/bErd/ bird	/uv/ of	/pEyz/ peas
/wEr/ were	/kwEyn/ queen	/pEys/ peace/piece
/wuns/ once	/kwik/ quick	/sidEy/ city
/wimen/ women	/fOwn/ phone	/ges/ guess
/w^men/ woman	/unyun/ onion	/skwAyr/ square

© Judy Thompson 2009

LettersStudent Page

Invisible Consonants©

You have learned the **40** sounds in English.
There are **24** consonant sounds and **16** vowel sounds.

Very good!

Your **foundation** of **sounds** is **nearly complete**.

There is **one** more thing you need to know about the **sounds of letters**.

There are consonant sounds that are pronounced – but not printed.

They are *invisible* consonants.

Invisible?

Invisible – look it up. It means *cannot be seen*.

in·vis·i·ble *adj.*
    1. Impossible to see; not visible. *Air is invisible.*

Yes, Invisible **Consonants**

 The scoop is, *you can't say vowel sounds together – they are both elastic!*

vowel**vowel**

What happens?

A little consonant sound gets slipped in between – stay tuned…

Invisible Consonants?!#

Who has ever heard of invisible consonants? No one, which is tragic. **Invisible consonants are one of the main reasons why non-native speakers don't sound like native speakers.** The good news is that they occur much more predictably than their silent cousins (more in Chapter Four).

If you try to pronounce vowel sounds together,   Owww Awww
you sound as if you have just been to the dentist.   Eyyy Owww

Vowel sounds have to be **separated** by **consonants** to be **pronounced.**

Other Languages

In other languages, syllables are constructed C·V·C or C·V in the first place because alternating *stopped* then *stretchy* sounds is the *easiest* way for humans to speak.

Chi/na, Ca/na/da, Nor/way, Ja/pan, Ger/ma/ny,
Bo/li/vi/a, Swe/den, I/ta/ly, Ko/re/a

Asian languages, in particular, prefer to stick closely to the easily pronounced C·V, C·V·C construction. English doesn't.

Native speakers talk the easiest way; they just **don't spell the way they talk.** When vowel sounds occur side by side (in separate syllables), native speakers slip consonants or *stopped sounds* in between so they can physically enunciate them. They fail to print them or let ESL students know what is happening.

It's not a secret.   Native speakers are **not aware** they do it.

Consonants Can Be Pronounced Together – tchst, ngbr, ghtsbr, rchcl ...

Does that look like English? Well, it is. English can string consonant sounds together with no problem. In pairs, they are *consonant blends* like **bl**ue and **st**ar. In compound words like ma**tchst**ick, Spri**ngbr**ook, Kni**ghtsbr**idge and Bi**rchcl**iffe, stringing consonant sounds together is easy. Pronouncing vowel sounds together is another story.

Vowels Can't Be Pronounced Together

The human mouth cannot physically produce back-to-back elastic vowel sounds. When two or three vowels are spelled together, they only represent one sound, like h**ea**d - /e/, l**au**gh - /a/ and delic**iou**s - /u/ – no pronunciation problem here. But when vowels are spelled beside each other and they belong to two different syllables (like poet - po/et and quiet - qui/et), they can't be pronounced, so the vowel sounds are separated with consonants that aren't printed, and the words are pronounced /po wet/ and /qui yet/. It's usually a **y** or a **w** that is spoken but not spelled – they are **invisible consonants.**

Rarely, other consonants are invisible.

/p/	Between **m** and **th**:	something - some**p**thing, warmth - warm**p**th
/g/	Before **k**:	pink - pin**g**k, pancake - pan**g**cake, banquet - ban**g**quet
/t/	In front of **z**:	pizza - pi**t**za, schizophrenic - schi**t**zophrenic

© Judy Thompson 2009

Invisible Consonants

Invisible consonants separate vowel sounds – usually **w** or **y**.

w	**y**
poem – po <u>w</u>em	**Leo the lion** – Le yo the li yon

Roses are red

*Roses are red,
violets are blue.
Sugar is sweet,
and so are you.*

It's almost always a **w** or a **y** that is spoken but **invisible**.

Sometimes,

/y/ at the beginning: uniform – <u>y</u>uniform

/w/ at the beginning: one – <u>w</u>un

Sometimes,

/w/ in the middle: poem – po<u>w</u>em

/y/ in the middle: cute – c<u>y</u>ute, few – f<u>y</u>ew

Don't worry about it. Words don't sound like they look, because *English is crazy*. That's all.

You are finished building your sound foundation!

CONGRATULATIONS!

www.thompsonlanguagecenter.com

Announcement
(Author Unknown)

The European Commission has just announced an agreement whereby English will be the official language of the EU rather than German, which was the other possibility. As a part of the negotiations, Her Majesty's Government conceded that English spelling had some room for improvement and has accepted a five-year phase-in plan that would be known as *Euro-English*.

In the first year, **s** will replace the soft **c**. Sertainly, this will make sivil servants jump with joy. The hard **c** will be dropped in favor of the **k**. This should klear up konfusion and keyboards kan have one less letter.

There will be growing publik enthusiasm in the second year, when the troublesome **ph** will be replaced with **f**. This will make words like *fotograf* 20% shorter.

In the third year, publik akseptanse of the new spelling kan be ekspekted to reach the stage where more komplikated changes are possible. Governments will enkorage the removal of double letters, which have always ben a deterent to akurate speling. Also, al wil agre that the horible mes of the silent 'e's in the language is disgraceful, and they should go away.

By the fourth year, peopl wil be reseptiv to steps such as replasing **th** with **z** and **w** with **v**. During ze fifs year, ze unesesary **o** kan be aplid to ozer kombinations of leters.

After zis fifs year, ve vill hav a realy sensibl riten styl. Zer vil be no mor trubl or difikultiz, and everyvun vil find it ezi to understand echozer.

Ze drem vil finaly kum tru! Unt ve vil tak over ze vorld!

What Students Should Know
Now I know my ABCs

As far as *speaking* goes, once they know their ABCs, students have gone about as far as they can go with the Latin alphabet. It's inadequate for the English language but it's what we've got. Learners need to know the names of the letters, spelling doesn't indicate pronunciation, accents are not necessarily a problem, and the *Thompson Vowel Chart* is a solid link to intelligibility. More on this in Chapter Two.

Laundry List

English doesn't sound like it looks.

What that means for the student is:

Learn to speak from listening.

Acquire English like a first language – from the beginning.

Chapter One
The Sounds of Letters

1. English is two separate languages – one *written* and one *spoken*.
2. The *written* alphabet does not match English sounds.
3. Spelling is random; any letter can represent any sound at any time.
4. English has two types of sounds:
    - Consonant sounds, which are stopped or restricted sounds
    - Vowel sounds, which are elastic or unrestricted sounds
5. Double consonants are usually pronounced as one, except cc and gg sometimes.
6. Vowel sounds are always separated by a consonant sound.
7. Consonant sounds are more strongly linked to spelling than vowels.
8. Vowel sounds are linked to **color names**.
9. Silent letters are letters you can see but represent no sound.
10. Invisible letters are clearly pronounced but there is no printed symbol.
11. No one can learn to speak English from reading it
12. The English Phonetic Alphabet (EPA) is a sound alphabet for *speaking* English with one symbol for each of the 40 sounds in the General American (GA) accent.

Way Too Difficult for ESL

1. At the army base, a bass was painted on the head of a bass drum.
2. They were too close to the door to close it.
3. The buck does funny things when the does are present.
4. The dove dove into the bushes.
5. He could lead if he would get the lead out.
6. A cat with nine lives lives next door.
7. She will mouth obscenities unless you stop her mouth.
8. After a number of injections, my jaw got number.
9. We polish the Polish furniture.
10. There was a row among the oarsmen about how to row.
11. A seamstress and a sewer fell down into a sewer line.
12. To help with planting, the farmer taught his sow to sow.
13. I shed a tear when I saw the tear in my clothes.
14. The wind was too strong to wind the sail.
15. The bandage was wound around the wound.
16. A rough-coated, dough-faced, thoughtful ploughmen strode through the streets of Scarborough; after falling into a slough, he coughed and hiccoughed.

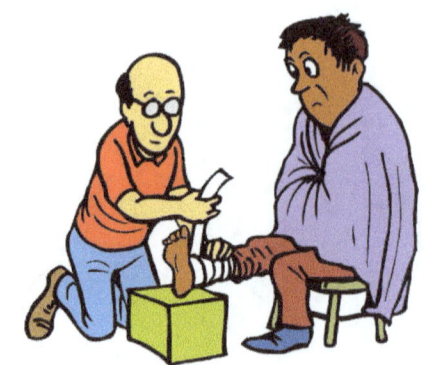

Chapter Two

WORDS

So You Want to Speak *Engwish?*

Syllables govern the world.
                                    John Seldon

CHAPTER TWO

So You Want to Speak *Engwish?*
or
Stop Worrying about your Accent

There are two types of languages. There are languages that rely on the clear pronunciation of each individual sound to convey meaning, known as *sound-based* languages. Asian languages, for example, are sound-based languages. Each and every symbol represents one and only one specific sound. If the sound is altered even a little bit, it is a different word.

In Chinese, the word for 4 is so close in pronunciation to the word for **death** that the number **4** is considered unlucky (like the number **13** in Western culture).

English is not like this. In English, letters can be horribly mispronounced or completely omitted with no meaning being lost, because English does not rely on the perfect production of individual sounds. Intelligibility in English relies on something else. English is a **stress-based language,** which means individual sounds are not particularly important. In North America, ask someone when their *birsday*, *birfday* or *birdday* is, and without hesitation, they will tell you the day they were born.

Example in Real Life
Three little old ladies meet for lunch at an Italian restaurant. The first lady has just been to the dentist. She asks the waiter for **spasgedi**. The next lady has had a stroke that has affected her speech. She orders **baskeddi**, and the third old darling has recently had a facelift. She asks for **spasghetta**. What do you think the waiter brought?

Three orders of **spaghetti**, exactly as if they had pronounced it correctly!

Students worry too much about making *exactly* the right sounds – but the truth is, in *Engwish,* **individual sounds aren't that important!**

English relies on **specific qualities** in **important syllables** for **meaning**.

The first step in being able to make oneself understood in conversation is being able to identify *syllables.*

Most students do this readily. Clapping hands or pounding on the desks as words are broken down into syllable units is a fun part of the exercise on the opposite page.

stu dent

tea cher

There is one and only one *vowel sound* in every syllable. Syllables are easy for students to identify. Have lower levels work in pairs to break words into syllables.

The Sounds of Words

Syllables, *STRESS* and Schwa

Syllables are the ***beats*** of ***words***.

pen   pencil

•   • •

pen   pencil
has 1 beat   has 2 beats

There is one **beat** for every vowel **sound**,

p**e**n   p**e**n c**i**l

not for every vowel.

•   •   •   • • •

sh**oe**   tr**ai**n   p**ie**   b**eau**tiful

It's one beat for every **vowel** sound.

Syllable Exercise – Beginner

Divide the following words into syllables.

     For example: red → red   student → stu / dent

blue	banana	fantastic	September
teacher	through	computer	beautiful
purple	China	guitar	television
Sunday	surprise	thirty	photography
green	believe	photograph	pronunciation

Stress

The second step in intelligibility is putting *stress* on important syllables. This is the cornerstone of *spoken* English. **Syllables are NOT all created equally.** Some **SY**llables are more im**POR**tant, and they are **STRESSED**.

No, not that kind of stress!

The **stress** students need to understand is about ***emphasis***.

Put the em**PHA**sis on the right syll**ABLE**.

No, No, No!

Put the **EM**phasis on the right **SY**llable!

Rule #2   English is a stress-based language.

If the **stress** is in the **wrong** place or missing, native English speakers **can't understand** you. **Three** specific **voice qualities** determine **stress** – **higher, louder, longer**.

 Banana has three syllables – **ba / na / na**

Syllables are not equally important.

It doesn't sound like **BA NA NA**. It sounds like ba **NA** na.

The first **na** is **HI**gher, **LOU**der and **LON**ger. It's ***stressed***.

If a learner asks an old white guy for a **BA** na na' or a ba na **NA**, the OWG doesn't know what they want and says,   What?

Then the learner is embarassed.

In ***written*** English, every letter in every syllable is important – it's called ***spelling***.

But in ***spoken*** English, only the important syllables are ***emphasized*** or ***stressed***.

Syllable Exercise Answer Key

blue	ba / na / na	fan / ta / stic	Sep / tem / ber
tea / cher	through	com / pu / ter	beau / ti / ful
pur / ple	Chi / na	gui / tar	te / le / vi / sion
Sun / day	sur / prise	thir / ty	pho / to / gra / phy
green	be / lieve	pho / to / graph	pro / nun / ci / a / tion

Stress

Stress = Important

Some **SY**llables are im**POR**tant and some are not.

Important syllables are:

LOUDER

and l o n g e r

than unimportant syllables.

Like calling the dog:

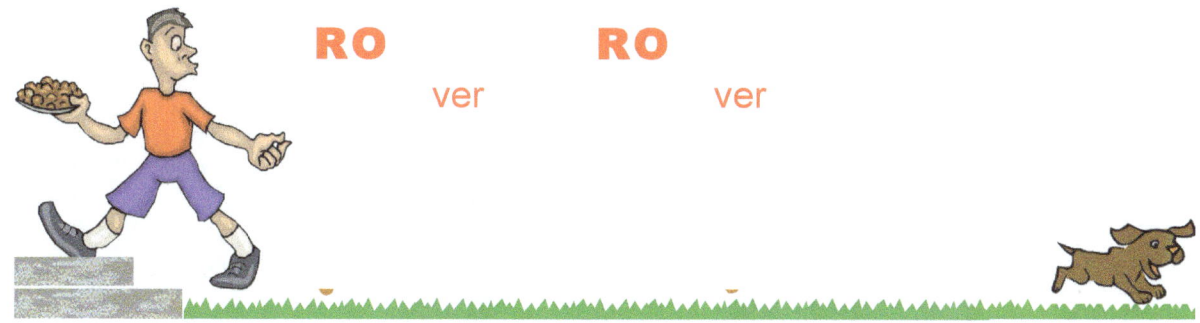

RO ver   **RO** ver

The words **pencil**, **baby** and **money** *look* one way, but they *sound* like:

PEN cil   **BA** by   **MO** ney

The first syllable in each of these words – **pen**cil, **ba**by and **mo**ney – is *stressed*.

Teacher Page   Words

WORD STRESS is EVerything

Review: Stressed syllables are **important** in English. They are **higher**, **louder** and **longer** than unstressed syllables. In this chapter, stressed syllables are printed in **CA**pital **LE**tters.

Lesson Idea

Three-Syllable Word Fun

Vowels sounds are *elastic* sounds. [Hook a big elastic on your thumbs and pull your hands apart on S T R E S S E D syllables.]

1st   2nd   3rd

1st	2nd	3rd
GEN tle man	ba **NA** na	kan ga **ROO**
HOS pi tal	com **PU** ter	un der **STAND**
TRI an gle	po **TA** to	en gin **EER**
GRAND mo ther	um **BRE** lla	Ja pa **NESE**

Keep a class set of elastic bands in your desk.
If students can get their hands to do it, their voices will follow.

What this Means for Students

The rubber band exercise is especially helpful for students who do not have stress in their languages, which can make them difficult to understand. (I WANT A BA NA NA.)

The Power of Word Stress

Stressed syllables are important because they *contain the meaning* in English.

Huh? Contain the meaning? To demonstrate the power of the stressed syllable for conveying meaning, students are presented with four *tiny tales* of different people asking for a drink of water. They ask for the water in very different ways – but the result is the same. Herein lies the power of the stressed syllable!

© Judy Thompson 2009

The Power of the *Stressed* Syllable

 If the King says:

    I'm parched. Do bring me a glass of **water**.

    Someone brings him water.

 If a businessperson says:

    Could I please have some **water**?

    Someone brings them water.

If a guy crawls in from the desert and says:

   Water, water.

    Someone brings him water.

It looks like **water** is the one important word in these three sentences. Look again:

If a toddler asks for a drink:

   Ma ma, **wa wa**.

    Someone brings her water.

The communication in each sentence is in the first syllable of **WA** ter.

The meaning in English is in **important syllables** and how they are **pronounced**. English is a **stress-based** language.

Teacher Page   Words

The Power of Stress Continued...

Change the Stress – Change the Meaning

record

Record   re**CORD**
<u>Noun</u>   <u>Verb</u>

relay

Relay   re**LAY**

produce

PROduce   pro**DUCE**

English is Crazy!

English looks like this: Farms produce produce.

The editor was content with the content.

A rebel likes to rebel.

English sounds like this: **FARMS** pro**DUCE** **PRO**duce.

The **ED**itor was con**TENT** with the **CON**tent.

A **RE**bel **LIKES** to re**BEL**.

Context tells where to put the stress to give meaning to a string of words.

Pair Work

Working in pairs with *speaking* exercises gives the students a chance to speak privately and listen exclusively.

The two most important things ESL students can acquire are **vocabulary** and **confidence**.

Confidence comes with practice and vocabulary comes from reading and conversation. ☺

80% Noun Rule and 60% Verb Rule

Nouns are **things.** In 80% of two-syllable nouns, the **stress** is on the **first syllable**.

They sound like **DA** da   (printed ● •)

       ANgel   **SU**gar   **DOC**tor

Verbs are **action** – 60% of two-syllable verbs sound like • ●
The **stress** is on the **second syllable**.

       re **LAX**   be **LIEVE**   sur **PRISE**

Stress Exercise – Intermediate

Mark the stress in each of the following one- or two-syllable words.

    one ●   two ● • or • ●   Hint: Say the words out loud.

● •

student	glasses	dentist
teacher	office	guitar
window	explain	brother
red	July	turquoise
yellow	April	length
purple	paper	people
delay	enjoy	discuss
employ	receive	record

www.thompsonlanguagecenter.com

Teacher Page   Words

Amazing

No matter how long a word is, there is only one major stressed syllable. One- and two-syllable words are easy to figure out, and when words get longer, it is still simple.

Stress and Accents

Germans speak English with a German accent. French people speak English with a French accent. Chinese speak English with a Chinese accent … first languages *interfere* with second language acquisition. French has a lot of second-syllable stress.

Ze French accent haz ze stress on ze end of ze word and ze phrase.

In sound-based languages where each letter represents one sound (like Korean or Punjabi), each syllable is equally important, which establishes the:

stea dy ev en sew ing ma chine rhy thm of these lan gua ges.

Answer Key

• .	• .	• .	• .	• .	. •
student	glasses	dentist	teacher	office	guitar
• .	. •	• .	•	. •	• .
window	explain	brother	red	July	turquoise
• .	• .	•	• .	• .	• .
yellow	April	length	purple	paper	people
. •	. •	. •	. •	. •	• . . •
delay	enjoy	discuss	employ	receive	record record

Exceptions: **It's only an 80% rule.**

July and guitar are both things, but they are not pronounced **JU ly** or **GUI tar**.

If the student has trouble with July and guitar, they probably didn't say the words out loud.

Change the stress, and native speakers won't understand you.

If you ask a native speaker for a **penCIL** or **moNEY**, they won't know what you want or they'll think you are French.

© Judy Thompson 2009

Amazing

It doesn't matter how long a word is, there is only **one** major stress syllable.

station	sta / tion	**2** syllables	**STA** tion
creation	cre / a / tion	**3** syllables	cre **A** tion
education	e / du / ca / tion	**4** syllables	e du **CA** tion
celebration	ce / le / bra / tion	**4** syllables	ce le **BRA** tion
congratulations	con / gra / tu / la / tions	**5** syllables	con gra tu **LA** tions

Incredible

It doesn't matter how long a word is, there is only **one really important** syllable.

The **meaning** of the whole **word** is in that **one stressed syllable**.

If you don't get that,
native speakers are not going to understand you.

You have to find the *stress* – and give the syllable some *bang!*

Teacher Page   Words

Syllable/Stress Exercise

Lesson Idea

Teacher note: The format of this exercise works for any vocabulary. Difficulty increases in each column. Repeat some words from previous pages because students are making a new *sound* base of language, separate from spelling. They will look back in the text to find the sounds of words they have seen before.

HOT TIP: Practice a few examples with students, but **DO IT WRONG!**

Put *stress* on each syllable, one at a time. Only one will 'sound right.'

    SPAghetti   spa**GHE**tti   spaghe**TTI**

Be silly so they can make mistakes, too – like a game.

When the students are all done the Syllable/Stress Exercise, have them say the words out loud – using their elastics. The stress is marked correctly in front of them, they have practiced with a partner, and there is safety in numbers. The group will drown out individual voices, but if someone isn't getting it, omniscient *super teacher ears* will pick that up.

Revisit the Spaghetti Story

The first lady ordered spasGEdi, the second ordered basKEddi, and the third, spasGHEtta. The waiter brings their lunch – three orders of **spaghetti** because the *stress* in each case was correct.

    • **•** •   • **•** •   • **•** •

    spaSGEdi   bas KE di   spa SGHE tta

**As long as the stress was in the right place,
the waiter could understand their orders.**

Lesson Idea: Numbers

This is a great time to look at the sounds of numbers. Without *stress*, 13 and 30 sound almost exactly the same, as do 14 and 40. This is why adult students have to drag their eight-year-olds shopping with them – because they can't pronounce numbers so that anyone can understand them. It's embarrassing. It's all in the stress.

    • **•**   **•** •

thirteen	/THEr TEYN/	thirty	/THER dEy/
fourteen	/for TEYN/	forty	/FOR dEy/
fifteen	/fif TEYN/	fifty	/FIF dEy/
sixteen	/siks TEYN/	sixty	/SIKS dEy/
seventeen	/se ven TEYN/	seventy	/SE ve nEy/
eighteen	/Ay TEYN/	eighty	/AY dEy/
nineteen	/nIyn TEYN/	ninety	/NIY nEy/

Like that… They'll thank you for straightening out that little mystery, maybe even buy you a coffee or a little present ☺

*Note that the unstressed **t** is /d/.

© Judy Thompson 2009   90

Words Student Page

Syllable / Stress Exercise

Divide the words into syllables and mark the stress.

Beginner	**Intermediate**	**Advanced**
angel	spaghetti	November
window	beautiful	Korea
purple	Halloween	India
paper	Canada	Malaysia
laugh	Saturday	Mexico
scissors	delicious	January
April	photograph	photography
ankle	fantastic	tomorrow
women	lion	Maria
beige	decided	education
begin	guitar	library
explain	Japanese	communicate
repeat	understand	television
July	hamburger	impossible
enjoy	thirty	thoroughly
color	thirteen	dictionary
police	fourteen	university
forgive	forty	congratulations
Japan	fifteen	responsibility
China	fifty	knowledgeable
surprise	agreement	pronunciation

www.thompsonlanguagecenter.com

Syllable/Stress Answer Key

● ·
an gel

● ·
win dow

● ·
pur ple

● ·
pa per

●
laugh

● ·
sci ssors

● ·
A pril

● ·
an kle

● ·
wo men

●
beige

· ●
be gin

· ●
ex plain

· ●
re peat

· ●
Ju ly

· ●
en joy

● ·
co lor

· ●
po lice

· ●
for give

· ●
Ja pan

● ·
Chi na

· ●
sur prise

· ● ·
spa ghe tti

● · ·
beau ti ful

· · ●
Ha llo ween

● · ·
Ca na da

● · ·
Sa tur day

· ● ·
de lic ious

● · ·
pho to graph

· ● ·
fan ta stic

● ·
li on

· ● ·
de ci ded

· ●
gui tar

· ● ·
Ja pa nese

· ● ·
un der stand

● · ·
ham bur ger

● ·
thir ty

· ●
thir teen

· ●
four teen

● ·
for ty

· ●
fif teen

● ·
fif ty

· ● ·
a gree ment

· ● ·
No vem ber

● · ·
Ko re a

● · ·
In di a

· ● · ·
Ma lay sia

● · ·
Mex i co

● · · ·
Ja nu a ry

· ● · ·
pho to gra phy

· ● ·
to mo rrow

· ● ·
Ma ri a

· · ● ·
e du ca tion

● · ·
li bra ry

· ● · ·
co mmu ni cate

· ● · ·
te le vi sion

· ● · ·
im po ssi ble

● · ·
tho rou ghly

● · · ·
dic tion a ry

· ● · · ·
u ni ver si ty

· · · ● ·
con gra tu la tions

· ● · · ·
re spon si bi li ty

· ● · ·
know led gea ble

· ● · · ·
pro nun ci a tion

Physical Training

Hook an elastic band between your thumbs and **stretch** your hands apart as you **stress** the **syllables OUT LOUD**.

Beginner	**Intermediate**	**Advanced**
AN gel	spa **GHE** tti	no **VEM** ber
WIN dow	**BEAU** ti ful	ko **RE** a
PUR ple	ha llow **EEN**	**IN** di a
PA per	**CA** na da	ma **LAY** sia
LAUGH	**SA** tur day	**ME** xi co
SCI ssors	de **LI** cious	**JAN** u a ry
A pril	**PHO** to graph	pho **TO** gra phy
AN kle	fan **TA** stic	to **MO** rrow
WO men	**LI** on	ma **RI** a
BEIGE	de **CI** ded	e du **CA** tion
be **GIN**	gui **TAR**	**LI** bra ry
ex **PLAIN**	ja pan **ESE**	co **MUN** ni cate
re **PEAT**	un der **STAND**	**TE** le vi sion
ju **LY**	**HAM** bur ger	im **PO** ssi ble
en **JOY**	**THIR** ty	**THO** rough ly
CO lor	thir **TEEN**	**DIC** tion a ry
po **LICE**	four **TEEN**	u ni **VER** si ty
for **GIVE**	**FOR** ty	con gra tu **LA** tions
ja **PAN**	fif **TEEN**	re spon si **BI** li ty
CHI na	**FIF** ty	**KNOW** ledge a ble
sur **PRISE**	a **GREE** ment	pro nun ci **A** tion

The Page that Doesn't Matter

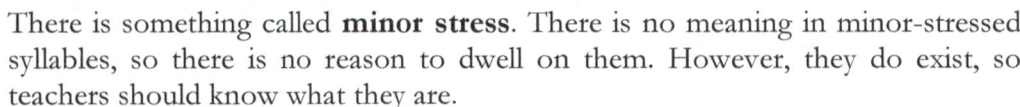

Note about minor stress: *It exists – but it doesn't matter.*

There is something called **minor stress**. There is no meaning in minor-stressed syllables, so there is no reason to dwell on them. However, they do exist, so teachers should know what they are.

- Minor stress syllables have a value less than stressed syllables.
- For example, **Judy** – /JUW dEy/ – two syllables – stress on the first syllable
- The important vowel sound here is /UW/ – blue
- The vowel sound in the second syllable is /Ey/ green. Not important.
- There is only one important syllable in each word.
- The second syllable has minor stress in /JUW dEy/.

For the purposes of this book, **only** major stressed and unstressed syllables are significant.

You can **rarely change the stress** without changing the meaning:

           • . .   . . •

magazine: MA ga zine   or   ma ga ZINE

           • . . .   . • . .

advertisement: AD ver tise ment or ad VER tise ment

           • . . .   . • . .

decorative: DE cor a tive or de COR a tive

 **Warning**   **Super Expert Advanced**   **Warning**

Different isn't Bad

Asian languages alternate consonants and vowels, beginning with consonants. In languages like Japanese, virtually all the syllables consist of a **consonant** followed by a **vowel**, as can be seen in such familiar brand names as *Toyota, Mitsubishi* and *Yamaha* — *To yo ta, Mi tshu bi shi, Ya ma ha*. Words can also end in consonants, but all syllables have equal weight. English is different as it will string consonants together in one word: '**p**lay, **str**eet, **tw**in, wa**sh**, ma**tchst**ick … and only some syllables are stressed.

When English words are used in Japanese, they get transformed in odd ways. *Boss,* for example, becomes *bosu* so that it does not end with a final consonant but with a vowel. The Japanese word *sutoraiki* turns back into the English word *strike* once its extra vowels are stripped off. English syllables can have consonants together anywhere in a word, including the end.

Stress in a Nutshell

Look what happens when the stress moves through parts of a word or phrase:

innocence	/**IN** uh sens/
in essence	/in **E** suhns/
in a sense	/in uh **SENS**/

 Warning   Beginners – Don't read this!   Warning

Super Expert Advanced Reading Exercise

Mark the major stressed syllable in the bolded words. (The clue is in the context.)

1. She was **content** with the **content** of the contract.
2. The record **contract** is void if they **contract** a disease.
3. They will **record** their present **record** live.
4. **Project** your voice when you present your **project**.
5. I **suspect** the guy with the gun in his hand was a **suspect**.
6. 'Live and let live' is my motto; I **protest** any kind of **protest**.
7. He's a repeat offender. I say **convict** the **convict**.
8. It's an **insult** to a man to **insult** his wife.
9. **Permit** me to buy you a fishing **permit** for your birthday.
10. Wheat is Canada's largest **export**; we **export** a lot every year.

How do You Know which Syllable to Stress?

You don't, not by reading – ba na na. There is no difference in print between the last two syllables, but there's a world of difference in pronunciation. If it's any comfort to learners, native speakers don't know how words are pronounced from reading them either. Since English letters don't correspond to sounds, everyone has to hear a word before they know how to pronounce it. But there is a way to figure out the stress.

[HINT: Move the stress – say it wrong.]

Try saying the stressed syllable in different places: **BA** na na – ba **NA** na – ba na **NA**. Students will likely notice which one **sounds right**. Have them begin to trust their memory of how the word sounds. With their new awareness of **stress**, it will get easier and easier to hear how stress works and when stress is wrong. It works the same way for everyone, so LISTENING TO A LOT OF ENGLISH is the way to learn how to speak it.

An *Ear* for the Language

It seems that native English speakers talk fast because learners don't have the *listening skill* to identify **important syllables**. Native speakers only pronounce *important* syllables clearly. Second language learners listen diligently to every little sound. IT'S NOT NECESSARY, and it's exhausting. Students listen too hard. When they relax and listen for the **high, loud, long** parts, life is easier.

It takes three months of immersion in a culture to develop an EAR for the language.

Super Advanced Answer Key

1. She was con**TENT** with the **CON**tent of the **CON**tract.
2. The record **CON**tract is void if they con**TRACT** a disease.
3. They will re**CORD** their present **RE**cord live.
4. Pro**JECT** your voice when you present your **PRO**ject.
5. I su**SPECT** the guy with the gun in his hand was a **SU**spect.
6. 'Live and let live' is my motto. I pro**TEST** any kind of **PRO**test.
7. He's a repeat offender. I say con**VICT** the **CON**vict.
8. It's an **IN**sult to a man to in**SULT** his wife.
9. Per**MIT** me to buy you a fishing **PER**mit for your birthday.
10. As Canada's largest **EX**port, we ex**PORT** a lot of wheat every year.

Words   Student Page

Stress Maze

1. **Connect** only the **three-syllable words** with the **stress** on the **second** syllable.

2. Enter the maze at **banana**.
3. Exit the maze at **direction**.

In ↓

banana ↓	library	January	office	beautiful
computer	believe	tomorrow	fantastic	agreement
spaghetti	September	decided	sometime	tomato
police	English	governor	plastic	example
scissors	manager	together	attraction	condition
possible	television	committee	operation	knowledge
through	insurance	opinion	holiday	vegetable
practice	suggestion	strength	classroom	mountain
opposite	delicious	Korea	remember	umbrella
language	because	observe	quality	direction ↓

Out

www.thompsonlanguagecenter.com 97

Teacher Page   Words

Schwa

Major Stress XXX
Important syllables have **major** stress and are really **important** in English. They are three times **longer**, **louder** and **higher** than unimportant syllables. They contain the meaning in English. Major stressed syllables are everything.

Minor Stress XX
Less important syllables have vowel sounds but no meaning. We don't care about them. Minor stressed syllables are nothing.

Unstressed X
Unimportant syllables carry no meaning and make almost no sound. They are so unimportant that native speakers don't bother to pronounce them, and the vowel sound of any unstressed syllable is reduced to a tiny grunt – /uh/. The name of this tiny grunt sound is *schwa*. English is a very lazy, grunty language. Schwa is everywhere.

Maze Answer Key 🗝

In						In				
banana	library	January	office	beautiful		banana	library	January	office	beautiful
computer	believe	tomorrow	fantastic	agreement		computer	believe	tomorrow	fantastic	agreement
spaghetti	September	decided	sometime	tomato		spaghetti	September	decided	sometime	tomato
police	English	governor	plastic	example		police	English	governor	plastic	example
scissors	manager	together	attraction	condition		scissors	manager	together	attraction	condition
possible	television	committee	operation	knowledge		possible	television	committee	operation	knowledge
through	insurance	opinion	holiday	vegetable		through	insurance	opinion	holiday	vegetable
practice	suggestion	strength	classroom	mountain		practice	suggestion	strength	classroom	mountain
opposite	delicious	Korea	remember	umbrella		opposite	delicious	Korea	remember	umbrella
language	because	observe	quality	direction		language	because	observe	quality	direction

Out   Out

© Judy Thompson 2009

Words   Student Page

/uh/

Remember /m<u>u</u>stErd/?

The sound /uh/ is like a
little, tiny baby mustard.

/u/

 /uh/

It's the tiniest sound the human voice can make.   /uh/

For such a tiny thing, it's amazing what it can do.

···

30% of all *spoken* English is /uh/.

The vowel sound of <u>all</u> <u>un</u>important syllables is /uh/.

Examples:
   banana really sounds like   /b<u>uh</u> NA n<u>uh</u>/

   potato really sounds like   /p<u>uh</u> TAY d<u>uh</u>/

   Canada really sounds like   /KA n<u>uh</u> d<u>uh</u>/

English sounds like  a little pig.

It makes lots of little grunts (/uh/) that don't mean anything.

 /uh/    /uh/

www.thompsonlanguagecenter.com   99

Teacher Page   Words

Schwa in Slow Motion

Students' speech will be more natural if they master the use of schwa.

Divide the following words into syllables and find the stressed syllable.

banana	ba na na	· ● · ba na na
request	re quest	· ● re quest
divide	di vide	· ● di vide
control	con trol	· ● con trol
unusual	un u su al	· ● · · un us u al

Listen closely to the unstressed syllable in each word. The sound of the unstressed syllables is /uh/.

		Sometimes spelled / ' /
ba NA na	b**uh** NA n**uh**	b**'** **na** n**'**
re QUEST	r**uh** QUEST	r**'** **quest**
di VIDE	d**uh** VIDE	d**'** **vide**
con TROL	c**uh**n TROL	c**'**n **trol**
un U su al	**uh**n Uw s**uh** w**uh**	**'**n **u** su **'**l

The vowel sound of all unimportant syllables is /uh/. The name of the sound is **schwa**.

No matter the vowel, – the first **a** in banana
                    – the first **e** in request
                    – the first **i** in divide
                    – the first **o** in control
                    – the first **u** in unusual

the **vowel sound** is /uh/ in unimportant syllables.   *You didn't believe me, did you?*

The vowel sound in **all unstressed syllables is reduced to schwa.**

Schwa is the most common sound in the English language. Any vowel or combination of vowels can be pronounced /uh/ when they occur in an unstressed syllable.

Pronunciation: uh EPA /uh/ The schwa sound is a teeny tiny /u/ mustard sound produced in the middle of the mouth / ' /. It is shorter and quieter than all other vowels. It is the most commonly occurring vowel sound in English!

© Judy Thompson 2009

The Magic Schwa Exercise

Fill in the blanks with the appropriate letters.

Beginner	Intermediate	Advanced
b_nan_	b_lieve	c_llapse
_bout	hosp_t_l	_partm_nt
d_lay	blank_t	c_ndit_n
r_lax	c_mplain	pois_n
min_te	dist_nt	c_noe
d_vide	stom_ch	inn_c_nce
t_day	s_ggest	ev_d_nce
J_ly	spec__l	s_spic___s
sec_nd	P_ru	d_lic___s
nat__n	vac_nt	curt__ns
p_lice	coll_ge	ox_g_n
dat_	pal_ce	acc_d_nt
mom_nt	lett_ce	exc_ll_nt
J_pan	Can_d_	imm_gr_nt
g__tar	b_lloon	p_sit__n
t_night	m_chine	sens_t_ve

What is the sound of **every** missing letter in this exercise?

 /uh/

The sound of every missing letter on this page is /uh/ – schwa.

 For bonus points, mark the major stressed syllables in the Magic Schwa exercise.

Teacher Page	Words

Ellipse

I usually avoid technical terms, but here is one. An unstressed syllable /uh/ that actually **disappears** in pronunciation is called an *ellipse*. Two syllables become one syllable when the unstressed syllable is dropped.

      • •   •

because   /b**uh** **CAUSE**/ → 👉 cause

good bye   /g**uh** **BYE**/ → 👉 bye

Three syllables become two syllables when the unstressed syllable is dropped.

family   /**FA** m**uh** ly/ → 👉 fam ly

probably /**PRO** b**uh** bly/ → 👉 pro bly…

But no meaning is lost –

like contractions: It's a small thing.

I am   I'm   **Ellipses** are everywhere.
you are you're   (Interesting, but the name is
cannot can't   not critically important.)

Answer Key 🗝

Beginner	Intermediate	Advanced
b<u>a</u>nana /b**uh**NA**nuh**/	bel<u>ie</u>ve /b**uh**LIEVE/	c<u>o</u>llapse /c**uh**LAPSE/
<u>a</u>bout /**uh**BOUT/	hosp<u>i</u>tal /HOsp**uh**t**uh**l/	<u>a</u>partm<u>e</u>nt /**uh**PARTm**uh**nt/
d<u>e</u>lay /d**uh**LAY/	blank<u>e</u>t /BLANk**uh**t/	cond<u>i</u>tion /c**uh**nDI**tuh**n/
r<u>e</u>lax /r**uh**LAX/	c<u>o</u>mplain /c**uh**mPLAIN/	pois<u>o</u>n /POIs**uh**n/
min<u>u</u>te /MIn**uh**te/	dist<u>a</u>nt /DIS**tuh**nt/	c<u>a</u>noe /c**uh**NOE/
d<u>i</u>vide /d**uh**VIDE/	stom<u>a</u>ch /STOm**uh**ch/	inn<u>o</u>cence /INn**uh**c**uh**nce/
t<u>o</u>day /t**uh**DAY/	sugg<u>e</u>st /s**uh**GEST/	ev<u>i</u>dence /Ev**uh**d**uh**nce/
J<u>u</u>ly /j**uh**LY/	spec<u>ia</u>l /SPEc**uh**l/	susp<u>i</u>cious /s**uh**SPIc**uh**s/
sec<u>o</u>nd /SEc**uh**nd/	P<u>e</u>ru /p**uh**RU/	del<u>i</u>cious /d**uh**LIc**uh**s/
nat<u>io</u>n /NA**tuh**n/	vac<u>a</u>nt /VAc**uh**nt/	curt<u>ai</u>ns /CURt**uh**ns/
p<u>o</u>lice /p**uh**LICE/	coll<u>e</u>ge /COll**uh**ge/	oxy<u>ge</u>n /Ox**uh**g**uh**n/
dat<u>a</u> /DAt**uh**/	pal<u>a</u>ce /PAl**uh**ce/	accid<u>e</u>nt /ACc**uh**d**uh**nt/
mom<u>e</u>nt /MOm**uh**nt/	lett<u>u</u>ce /LEtt**uh**ce/	excell<u>e</u>nt /EXc**uh**ll**uh**nt/
J<u>a</u>pan /j**uh**PAN/	Can<u>a</u>d<u>a</u> /CAn**uh**d**uh**/	immigr<u>a</u>nt /IMm**uh**gr**uh**nt/
g<u>u</u>itar /g**uh**TAR/	ball<u>oo</u>n /b**uh**LOON/	p<u>o</u>sition /p**uh**SI**tuh**n/
t<u>o</u>night /t**uh**NIGHT/	m<u>a</u>chine /m**uh**CHINE/	sensit<u>i</u>ve /SENs**uh**t**uh**ve/

© Judy Thompson 2009

Words   Student Page

Disappearing Syllables

Sometimes unstressed syllables /uh/ *disappear*.

Wait a sec.

2 syllables → **1 syllable**

second – se c**uh**nd   'sec'

3 syllables → **2 syllables**

family – fa m**uh** ly   fam ly

family

chocolate – cho c**uh** late   choc late

chocolate

4 syllables → **3 syllables**

vegetable – ve g**uh** ta ble   veg ta ble

vegetable

Sometimes, many syllables disappear.

airplane   3   aeroplane   2   airplane   1   plane

Very, Very Advanced Unimportant Exercise

This material is *not* important, so don't do it if you don't want to. Find the unstressed syllable that disappears from these words; then figure out the sound of the words.

second	brother	I am
because	camera	you are
good bye	mirror	he is
family	mystery	cannot
probably	favorite	they are
chocolate	Margaret	will not
vegetable	Niagara	have not

www.thompsonlanguagecenter.com

Too Much Information

The **schwa story** is another nail in the English-doesn't-sound-like-it-looks coffin.

Students don't have to be able to pronounce schwa or even recognize it. What they have to understand is that schwa is one of the main reasons why they can't reconcile the sounds they hear with the vocabulary they have learned. They expect to hear the words they have studied, and they never will. English is mostly /uh/ /uh/ /uh/ – tiny grunts.

The good news is that native speakers grunt in the place of *meaningless* syllables. Grunting is the clue that WE DON'T HAVE TO PAY ATTENTION TO THEM.

So much of *spoken* English is insignificant mumbling. The important parts are high, loud and long – so students will begin to catch them if they are taught what to listen for!

English is a Stress-Based Language

Students exhaust themselves listening to every little sound, and it isn't necessary. They wonder all the time, what did he say? And they never figure it out. Listening becomes much **easier** once students learn to listen for **WORD STRESS**. It takes practice, but their quality of life vastly improves once they get the hang of it. Encourage students to stop worrying so much. They'll get it after they have listened to enough English.

85% of our learning is derived from listening.
Harvey Mackay

Context and Word Stress Practice
Some *Real* English to Wrap Your Tongue Around

1. The soldier decided to desert his dessert in the desert.
2. The entrance to a mall fails to entrance me.
3. I spent last evening evening out a pile of dirt.
4. How can I intimate this to my most intimate friend?
5. The insurance for the invalid was invalid.
6. I did not object to the object.
7. There is no time like the present to present the present.
8. A farm can produce produce.
9. The dump was so full it had to refuse more refuse.
10. I had to subject the subject to a series of tests.

Answer Key

second	/**SE** c**uh**nd/	sec	brother	/ **BRO** th**uh**r /	bro	I am	I'm
because	/b**uh CAUSE**/	cause	camera	/**CAM uh** ra /	cam ra	you are	you're
good bye	/g**uh**d **BYE**/	bye	mirror	/**MIR uh**r/	mir	he is	he's
family	/**FA** m**uh** ly/	fam ly	mystery	/**MY**st**uh** ry/	mys try	cannot	can't
probably	/**PRO** b**uh**b ly/	pro bly	favourite	/**FA** v**uh** rite/	fav rite	they are	they're
chocolate	/**CHO** c**uh** late/	choc late	Margaret	/**MAR** g**uh** ret/	Marg ret	will not	won't
vegetable	/**VE** g**uh** ta ble/	veg ta ble	Niagara	/nI **YA** g**uh** ra/	Niag ra	have not	haven't

© Judy Thompson 2009

What the Student Needs to Know about Words

Learn lots of them.

Words are the voice of the heart.
Chinese Proverb

If you are going to speak English, you need VOCABULARY.

Study the *stress pattern* of words at the same time as the spelling, to learn both *spoken* English and *written* English at the same time.

TAble, **DESK**, com**PU**ter ...

WAllet

refe**REE**

ROOster

gradu**A**tion

XYlophone

CHESTnuts

trom**BONE**

muske**TEERS**

Laundry List

English is a Stress-based Language.

What that means for the student is:

Listen for *word stress* and speak with *word stress*.

If you speak without *stress*, people will not understand you.

Chapter Two
The Sounds of Words

1. The building blocks of words are **syllables**.
2. Syllables are defined by vowel sounds.
3. There is one and only one vowel sound in every syllable.
4. In speaking, there are important, less important, and unimportant syllables.
5. Important syllables are stressed.
6. Three voice qualities create syllable stress: higher, louder and longer.
7. There is only one most important syllable in any word, no matter how long the word.
8. The vowel sound in unimportant syllables is a tiny grunt called schwa – **uh**
9. Less important syllables have a vowel sound, but no one cares, they are unimportant.
10. Intelligibility and meaning in English are a function of context and stressed syllables.
11. English is a stress-based language.

Chapter Three

SENTENCES

Not All Words are Created Equally

*Man is a creature who lives not upon bread alone,
but primarily by catchwords.*

Robert Louis Stevenson

Teacher Page   Sentences

CHAPTER THREE

Not All Words are Created Equally
or
There is No Such Thing as Grammar

Like the important and unimportant syllables we learned about in Chapter Two, sentences are made of both important and unimportant words. Important words are called **content** words. They are important for *speaking*. Just like important syllables, important words are *stressed* and carry meaning.

Unimportant words are called **function** words. They are the tiny little words that are not as important for *speaking* as they are for *writing*. All words are either **content** words or **function** words. Students need to know they can be understood by simply saying only content words.

Me Tarzan. You Jane.
Got it.

Grammar doesn't need to be perfect for people to understand.

Learners are *crippled* by *two myths*:

1. They believe their **accent** impedes understanding – and it usually doesn't (Chapter One).
2. They believe their **grammar** isn't good enough – and it is (Chapter Three).

Teachers need to understand grammar is useful for writing only, it impedes speaking ability. Focus on grammar in language classes was because it is easy to mark. Current trends are experiential learning (learn by doing vs. studying about) and facilitation where mistakes are part of the process. More freedom, less shame.

The Sounds of Sentences

In **writing**, every letter and every word are important.

The money is **o**n the wallet.

The money is **i**n the wallet.

In English class, you probably learned:

Hello. How are you? My name is Rick.

Hello, Rick. My name is Susan.

Nice to meet you, Susan.

Nice to meet you, Rick.

24 words

And that's fine for *writing* but …

Speaking is different.

A guy sticks out his hand and says,

Rick

The woman shakes his hand and says,

Susan

2 words

Rule #3   **IMPORTANT WORDS can be enough information.**

For students learning to **speak**, there are **IMPORTANT WORDS**, and then there is *fluff*.

Rick and **Susan** are the most important words in this conversation. The rest is *fluff*.

Conversation is heavily supported by context and gestures.

Content Words

Important words are called content words. They **contain** the meaning. *Spoken* English *stresses* content words. These are nouns, verbs, adverbs, adjectives, negatives, intensifiers and two-syllable prepositions. Content words are the words in capital letters in a title. Stressing content words is how native speakers communicate – even though most of them don't know it.

Teach the parts of speech appropriate to the learner's level.

Content words:

Begin with   **Nouns:** (person, place or thing) cat, house, city, mother, country
                  Verbs: (action words) sing, play, walk, enjoy, believe, express

Then   **Adverbs**: (answer where, when, or how) there, today, quickly
                  Adjectives: (describe nouns and adjectives) blue, big, funniest, beautiful

Finally   **Negatives:** (opposite of positive) no, not, never
                  Intensifiers: (stronger adverb or adjective) rather, very, too, extremely

Pure Communication

Here are some samples of successful statements from beginner students.

I come back book.
(Did she return the book to the library or not?)

Lost my test drive.
(Did he pass his driver's test?)

You no class Friday?
(Is Good Friday a school holiday?)

Teacher you me washroom?
The answer is Yes.
(I don't have to go. ☺)

There is enough information in **back book** to know she returned it, **lost test** to know he's going to have to take it over, **no class** to find out if Good Friday is a holiday, and **washroom** for her to get permission to powder her nose.

Learners' grammar doesn't have to be perfect for native speakers to understand them.

The finest language is mostly made up of simple unimposing words.
                                                    George Eliot

Sentences Student Page

Important Words

Important words are **content words**. They are nouns and verbs. In this chapter, CONTENT WORDS are PRINTED in CAPITAL LETTERS.

Beginner: NOUNS, or *THINGS,* are IMPORTANT.

CAR   BOOK   HOUSE   TREE   LOVE

VERBS, or *ACTIONS,* are IMPORTANT.

RUN   JUMP   KICK   DANCE   READ

CONTENT WORDS are STRONG MESSAGES on their own – without grammar.

NO! HELP. FIRE. STOP. TAXI. HUSBAND. COME. GIVE...

Be brave.

Try saying nouns and verbs to strangers.

JUMP!

It will be O.K.

This is all beginner students need to know.

www.thompsonlanguagecenter.com   111

Right or Wrong? # @ $!

It's not about right or wrong. It's about being effective. Was there understanding or not? If there was understanding, then the communication was successful. Learners can use only nouns and verbs in speaking to get their message across. It's not perfect, but it works.

I have always thought you could learn to get around in any language if you could concentrate on about thirty well-chosen verbs, a couple of dozen nouns, a few pleasantries and some basic sense of word order.

Alan Alda in his autobiography

Alan Alda was right.

The first four words students need in any language ☺ :

Hello   Please   Thanks   Restroom

Function Words - Fluff

Written English requires **function words.** These are articles, conjunctions, pronouns, the verb *to be*, auxiliary (helping) verbs, modals, and one-syllable prepositions. Function words are *grammar* words and are important in *written* English.

Function words are:

Articles	a, an, the
Conjunctions	and, but, or
Pronouns	it, you, they, them, your
Verb *To Be*	am, are, is
Modals	could, should, will
Auxiliary verbs	have, has, do, does
One-syllable prepositions	in, on, at, to

The vowel sound of function words is /uh/ – schwa.

This is why *spoken* English sounds like mumbling – not because native speakers are tipsy, but because of schwa. It is mumbling!

Teacher Note: Two-Syllable Prepositions

There is an **overriding rule** in English: In words larger than one syllable, some syllable must be stressed. For example, **between** is a preposition and prepositions aren't important, but since it is two syllables, it must have stress: be TWEEN – /b**uh** TWEEN/

© Judy Thompson 2009

Unimportant Words

Unimportant words are **function words**. They are the little tiny words that stick important words together in *writing,* but they are not important in *speaking*:

a, an, the, in, on, at, with, or, but, to, will, have, can, am, are, you, them, they, could, may…

Function words are *grammar* words for *writing*. They are glue. They are not necessary for *speaking*.

Function words are ***writing*** words.

In *speaking,* function words are reduced to little grunts –

/uh/, /uh/, /uh/

So, English sounds like this

you	/yuh/	ya	You know?	Ya know?
to	/tuh/	ta	four to eight	4 ta 8
do	/duh/	da	Do you think so?	da ya think so?
a	/uh/	a	a cup of coffee	a cup a coffee
of	/uh/	a	a bottle of water	a bottle a water
an	/uhn/	un	It's an apple.	It's un apple
and	/uhn/	un	salt and pepper	salt un pepper
what	/whuh/	wa	What is up?	wa sup?

No Picture, No Sound

Native speakers don't pronounce words they can't make a mental picture of. What is the image of **a** or **of** or **the**…? There isn't one.
   If there is no **picture,** they are **not pronounced**.

All function words are <u>un</u>important for *speaking*.

The same as unimportant syllables,

the vowel sound of function words is /uh/.

English looks like this: English sounds like this:

a cup of coffee   uh CUP uh COffee

and **Coffee** means exactly the same thing.
Grammar is not important in *speaking* English!

Teacher Page   Sentences

What this Means for the Student

Knowing the importance of **content** words and the unimportance of function words means **three very significant** things for the student:

1. *Speaking* English is **easier** than they thought – use **important words**.
2. *Listening* is **easier** than they **thought** – listen for **important words**.
1. *Writing* is much more **difficult** than *speaking* because there are so many grammar rules and tiny little grammar words.

Important words are *stressed.* **Unimportant words** are *grunted.*   uh

WOLVES EAT SHEEP

Read each sentence out loud and clap on each content word. There are **three content words** in each sentence so each sentence **takes the same amount of time** for a native speaker to say. The last sentence, with seven *written* words, takes the same amount of time to say as the first one with three. Try it. Say them out loud and clap. Read the sentences with the class, slowly and steadily. Students won't be able to do the last two sentences; their first language has them pronounce every letter – native speakers do not.

Number of *writing* words		Number of *speaking* words
3	WOLVES EAT SHEEP	3
4	the WOLVES EAT SHEEP	3
5	the WOLVES EAT the SHEEP	3
6	the WOLVES will EAT the SHEEP	3
6	the WOLVES have EATen the SHEEP	3
7	the WOLVES will have EATen the SHEEP	3

Sounds like: thuh WOLVES wuhl huv EATuhn thuh SHEEP
Also written: th' WOLVES w'l h'v EAT'n th' SHEEP

Native speakers mumble. Students exhaust themselves listening too hard when they really only have to listen to half the words that are spoken. Learners needn't worry when they don't catch everything. Content words are **higher**, **longer** and **louder** than function words.

Important words are **spoken clearly.**

When learners stop worrying that they've missed something, they begin to hear everything.

© Judy Thompson, 2009

Sentences   Student Page

Content or Function?

Print a **C** for **content words** and an **F** for **function words** on the line beside each word. The first few are done for you:

a	F	kick	_	with	_	have	_
an	F	tree	_	or	_	can	_
three	C	sing	_	but	_	am	_
car	C	laugh	_	read	_	help	_
and	_	wife	_	may	_	might	_
run	_	to	_	book	_	love	_
house	_	will	_	of	_	you	_
fire	_	as	_	jump	_	them	_
on	_	cry	_	should	_	wolf	_
at	_	could	_	does	_	sheep	_
bus	_	in	_	give	_	them	_
are	_	stop	_	hour	_	lunch	_

www.thompsonlanguagecenter.com

Teacher Page   Sentences

FUN with CONTENT and FUNCTION WORDS

Native speakers don't register function words even when read, which makes for gimmicky little fun things found on the Internet, like this:

Count every **F** in the following text.

FINISHED FILES ARE THE RESULT OF YEARS OF SCIENTIFIC STUDY COMBINED WITH THE EXPERIENCE OF YEARS...

HOW MANY?
    Native speakers will say 3.
    ESL students will say 6.
    The ESL students will be right.

Really, go back and try to find the 6 Fs.

Native speakers don't process **function words**. Since they **aren't important,** they skip right over them.

ESL students count 6 **F**s because of their first language learning where every letter is important. They think it's a silly question.

Answer Key

a	F	kick	C	with	F	have	F
an	F	tree	C	or	F	can	F
three	C	sing	C	but	F	am	F
car	C	laugh	C	read	C	help	C
and	F	wife	C	may	F	might	F
run	C	to	F	book	C	love	C
house	C	will	F	of	F	you	F
fire	C	as	F	jump	C	them	F
on	F	dance	C	should	F	wolf	C
at	F	could	F	does	F	sheep	C
bus	C	in	F	give	C	them	F
are	F	stop	C	hour	C	lunch	C

© Judy Thompson 2009

Sentences　　　　　　　　Student Page

Similes

Crossword Puzzle

ACROSS
- 4 As silly as a
- 6 As sick as a
- 10 As hungry as a
- 12 As playful as a
- 13 As strong as an
- 14 As quiet as a
- 16 As hairy as an
- 17 As gentle as a
- 19 As eager as a

DOWN
- 1 As fat as a
- 2 As busy as a
- 3 As free as a
- 5 As drunk as a
- 7 As wise as an
- 8 As blind as a
- 9 As proud as a
- 10 As big as a
- 11 As sly as a
- 15 As slow as a
- 18 As stubborn as a

Teacher Page   Sentences

The Function Word Phenomenon

Read out loud the text inside the triangle below.

If you are a native English speaker, you probably said,

A bird in the bush.

If English is your second language, you probably said,

A bird in the the bush.

The ESL students are right.

Native speakers don't register function words well.

Answer Key

What does the phrase *sound* like?

1.	As fat as a pig	uhz **FAT** uhz uh **PIG**
2.	As busy as a bee	uhz **BUSY** uhz uh **BEE**
3.	As free as a bird	uhz **FREE** uhz uh **BIRD**
4.	As silly as a goose	uhz **SILLY** uhz uh **GOOSE**
5.	As drunk as a skunk	uhz **DRUNK** uhz uh **SKUNK**
6.	As sick as a dog	uhz **SICK** uhz uh **DOG**
7.	As wise as an owl	uhz **WIZE** uhz uhn **OWL**
8.	As blind as a bat	uhz **BLIND** uhz uh **BAT**
9.	As proud as a peacock	uhz **PROUD** uhz uh **PEA**COCK
10. Across.	As hungry as a wolf	uhz **HUN**GRY uhz uh **WOLF**
10. Down	As big as a whale	uhz **BIG** uhz uh **WHALE**
11.	As sly as a fox	uhz **SLY** uhz uh **FOX**
12.	As playful as a kitten	uhz **PLAY**FUL uhz uh **KIT**TEN
13.	As strong as an ox	uhz **STRONG** uhz uhn **OX**
14.	As quiet as a mouse	uhz **QUI**ET uhz uh **MOUSE**
15.	As slow as a snail	uhz **SLOW** uhz uh **SNAIL**
16.	As hairy as an ape	uhz **HARR**Y uhz uhn **APE**
17.	As gentle as a lamb	uhz **GEN**TLE uhz uh **LAMB**
18.	As stubborn as a mule	uhz **STUB**BORN uhz uh **MULE**
19.	As eager as a beaver	uhz **EA**GER uhz uh **BEA**VER

© Judy Thompson 2009

Content Word Hunt

Beginner:
Find the *missing content words* in each of these expressions.

Intermediate:
Find the *missing content words* and *stress* them.

Advanced:
Find the *stressed syllables* in the *missing content words*.

1. 60 **s** in a **m:** 60 seconds in a minute   60 SECuhnds uhn uh MINuht
2. 24 **h** in a **d** _____
3. 7 **d** in a **w** _____
4. 52 **w** in a **y** _____
5. 52 **c** in a **d** _____
6. 12 **m** in a **y** _____
7. 12 **e** in a **d** _____
8. 4 **q** in a **d** _____
9. 5 **n** in a **q** _____
10. 2 **p** in a **q** _____
11. 2 **w** on a **b** _____
12. 3 **w** on a **t** _____
13. 100 **cm** in a **m** _____
14. 12 **i** in a **f** _____
15. 360 **d** in a **c** _____
16. 90 **d** in a **r a** _____
17. 0° **C** is **f** _____
18. 10 **f** and 10 **t** _____

www.thompsonlanguagecenter.com

Teacher Page   Sentences

The Natural Rhythm of *Speaking* English

• • ● • • ● • • ● • • ●

In English, stressed and unstressed words alternate in a fairly regular pattern of a few function • • words, then a content word ● , almost creating a *rhythm* in English.

Native speakers commonly speak using this pattern.

From *The Cat in the Hat* to *Jingle Bells*, reading poetry out loud is the perfect place to practice the rhythm of English.

ta da **DAH**   ta da **DAH**   ta da **DAH**

A Perfect Example

The Best of Whatever You Are over on the student's page is part of an inspirational poem written by Douglas Malloch that was included in a speech given by Dr. Martin Luther King, Jr., to a group of students at Barrett Junior High School in Philadelphia on October 26, 1967, six months before he was assassinated.

Answer Key 🗝

1.	60 **s** in a **m**	60 <u>seconds</u> in a <u>minute</u>	60 **SEC**onds 'n uh **MIN**ute
2.	24 **h** in a **d**	24 <u>hours</u> in a <u>day</u>	24 **HOURS** 'n uh **DAY**
3.	7 **d** in a **w**	7 <u>days</u> in a <u>week</u>	7 **DAYS** 'n uh **WEEK**
4.	2 **w** in a **y**	52 <u>weeks</u> in a <u>year</u>	52 **WEEKS** 'n uh **YEAR**
5.	52 **c** in a **d**	52 <u>cards</u> in a <u>deck</u>	52 **CARDS** 'n uh **DECK**
6.	2 **m** in a **y**	12 <u>months</u> in a <u>year</u>	12 **MONTHS** 'n uh **YEAR**
7.	12 **e** in a **d**	12 <u>eggs</u> in a <u>dozen</u>	12 **EGGS** 'n uh **DO**zen
8.	4 **q** in a **d**	4 <u>quarters</u> in a <u>dollar</u>	4 **QUAR**ters 'n uh **Do**llar
9.	5 **n** in a **q**	5 <u>nickels</u> in a <u>quarter</u>	5 **NI**ckels 'n uh **QUAR**ter
10.	2 **p** in a **q**	2 <u>pints</u> in a <u>quart</u>	2 **PINTS** 'n uh **QUART**
11.	2 **w** o a **b**	2 <u>wheels</u> on a <u>bicycle</u>	2 **WHEELS** 'n uh **BI**cycle
12.	3 **w** on a **t**	3 <u>wheels</u> on a <u>tricycle</u>	3 **WHEELS** 'n uh **TRI**cycle
13.	100 **cm** in a **m**	100 <u>centimeters</u> in a <u>meter</u>	100 **CENTI**meters 'n uh **ME**ter
14.	12 **i** in a **f**	12 <u>inches</u> in a <u>foot</u>	12 **IN**ches 'n uh **FOOT**
15.	360 **d** in a **c**	90 <u>degrees</u> in a <u>right angle</u>	90 de**GREES** 'n uh **RIGHT ANG**le
16.	90 **d** in a **r a**	360 <u>degrees</u> in a <u>circle</u>	360 de**GREES** 'n uh **CIR**cle
17.	0° **c** is **f**	0 <u>degrees</u> <u>centigrade</u> is <u>freezing</u>	0 de**GREES CEN**tigrade 's **FREE**zin
18.	10 **f** and 10 **t**	10 <u>fingers</u> and 10 <u>toes</u>	10 **FIN**gers 'n 10 **TOES**

© Judy Thompson 2009

The Best of Whatever You Are

If you can't be a pine at the top of the hill,
    be a shrub in the valley, but be
the best little shrub on the side of the hill.
    Be a bush if you can't be a tree.

If you can't be a highway, just be a trail.
    If you can't be a sun, be a star.
For it isn't by size that you win or fail.
    Be the best of whatever you are.

Taken from a poem by Douglas Malloch

Try it out loud. Clap your hands at the stress dots.

The Best of Whatever You Are

If you can't be a pine at the top of the hill,

be a shrub in the valley, but be

the best little shrub on the side of the hill.

Be a bush if you can't be a tree.

If you can't be a highway, just be a trail.

If you can't be a sun, be a star.

For it isn't by size that you win or fail.

Be the best of whatever you are.

Final version, with lots of reading-out-loud support:

The **BEST** of What**EVER** You **ARE**

If you **CAN'T** be a **PINE** at the **TOP** of the **HILL**,

be a **SHRUB** in the **VA**lley, but **BE**

the **BEST** little **SHRUB** on the **SIDE** of the **HILL**.

Be a **BUSH** if you **CANT** be a **TREE**.

If you **CANT** be a **HIGH**way, **JUST** be a **TRAIL**.

If you **CANT** be a **SUN**, be a **STAR**.

For it **ISN'T** by **SIZE** that you **WIN** or **FAIL**.

Be the **BEST** of what **Ever** you **ARE**.

Some Facts about FOCUS

Content words are stressed, and **function** words **can be stressed** if they are **important** for **meaning**. The focus of a simple statement changes by putting stress on function words.

His book is in her desk.

Whose book?	**HIS** book is in her desk.
His what?	His **BOOK** is in her desk.
Are you sure?	His book **IS** in her desk.
Where on her desk?	His book is **IN** her desk.
Whose desk?	His book is in **HER** desk.
Where in her purse?	His book is in her **DESK**.

Exaggerate stress on a word or idea for special focus.

Once the students understand what stress is and how it works, listening becomes easier and more effective.

Students are surprised to learn that conversation in English is much easier than *writing*. If they are having difficulty making a native speaker understand them, it's lack of **word stress not** lack of **grammar** that is the **problem**.

Sentences   Student Page

Important Words

Beginner: Match the content words.
Caution: There are two extra nouns.

Head is to
As hand is to

Father is to
As mother is to

House is to
As barn is to

Winter is to
As spring is to

cow
son
glove
summer
hat
person
water
autumn
daughter
tree

Intermediate: Read the poem below out loud.
The pattern is 4 stresses in the first sentence and 3 in the second: 4, 3, 4, 3...

Mary had a Little Lamb

Mary had a little lamb,
    its fleece was white as snow;
and everywhere that Mary went,
    the lamb was sure to go.

He followed her to school one day;
    that was against the rule.
It made the children laugh and play
    to see a lamb at school.

Advanced: Keep reading about Mary and the lamb.

And so the teacher turned it out
    but still it lingered near
and waited patiently about
    'till Mary did appear.

"Why does the lamb love Mary so?"
    the eager children cry.
"Why Mary loves the lamb, you know,"
    the teacher did reply.

Sarah Hale 1830

www.thompsonlanguagecenter.com

People Are Unaware

Native English speakers don't know it, but they favor a regular rhythm when they speak. They naturally condense function words and enunciate content words: **ta da DAH** is the effect. Something else they do all the time without thinking is ***guess from printed clues***.

They have to guess since *written* English is an

Answer Key

Head is to hat   as hand is to glove.
Father is to son   as mother is to daughter.
House is to person   as barn is to cows.
Winter is to summer   as spring is to autumn.

water and tree are extra

Mary had a Little Lamb

MAry HAD a LIttle LAMB,

its FLEECE was WHITE as SNOW;

and EVeryWHERE that MAry WENT,

the LAMB was SURE to GO.

He FOllowed HER to SCHOOL ONE DAY;

that WAS aGAINST the RULE.

It MADE the CHILdren LAUGH and PLAY

to SEE a LAMB at SCHOOL,

and SO the TEAcher TURNED it OUT,

but STILL it LINgered NEAR,

and WAIted PAtientLY aBOUT

Till MAry DID aPPEAR.

"Why DOES the LAMB LOVE MAry SO?"

the EAger CHILdren CRY.

"Why MAry LOVES the LAMB, you KNOW,"

the TEAcher DID rePLY.

© Judy Thompson 2009

ta da DAH

ta da **DAH** is the natural rhythm of English. *Speaking* too perfectly sounds odd.

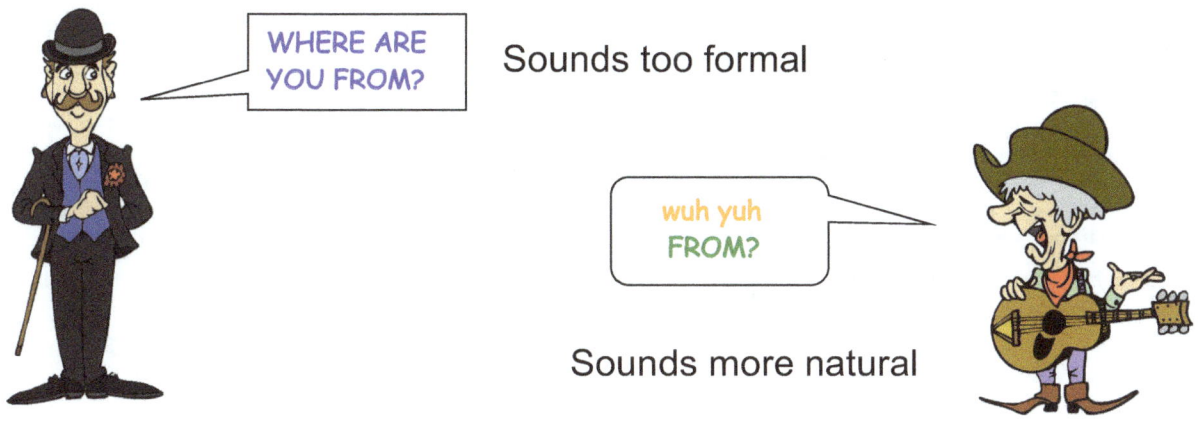

Sounds too formal

Sounds more natural

Natural *speaking* is **not** clear. With the help of context, gestures and content words, native English speakers **guess** what is being said.

Written English is an Optical Illusion

(Look up *optical illusion*.)

Young woman or old woman?

Where are the black dots?

Old man or young woman?

It is not as it seems. ***Written*** **English is a secret code.** Even **if** you can understand what it means, you aren't sure what it sounds like. If you understand what you hear, you don't know how to spell it.

Teacher Page   Sentences

In Case They Ask

Note about **minor** word stress:

It exists, but it doesn't matter.

Just like minor stressed syllables that aren't very important, there are minor stressed words that aren't very important either. They have vowel sounds that are not /**uh**/ but they still don't carry much meaning. They have a value less than focus words.

WH? Question Words

What, Where, When, Why, Who and *How* get a small  of stress in *speaking* – just enough WH to indicate Give me information before the speaker ellipses into the rest of the sentence.

What did he say?   Whuh dɪy **SAY**

Demonstratives

This, that, these and *those* get the smallest of as well.

These are for Bob.   THEyzerfer **BOB**

It's technical, confusing and not particularly empowering. We aren't going to dwell on it, but in case someone asks, there it is. Minor stress exists, but there is no reason to worry about it. In this book, there are only important and unimportant words.

Back to Business

To speak English, students have to give up reading and **listen**. This is a recording… They have to listen to hours of English every day even if they don't understand – *especially* if they don't understand. Once they have spent lots of time just listening to English, one day it stops sounding like a big blurry mumble, and they begin to be able to identify the important words.

English is indistinct and requires a lot of guessing – even when it's your first language.

HOT TIP

Have your students listen to the weather on the radio every morning – it repeats every half hour. Have them watch it on TV, too. They can look out the window to verify what they have heard.

⁝ wakinna **weather** arweinfor **today?**
Ihopeweseealittle **sunshine**
lateronbutprobly **not** ⁝

Don't let them give up. The students will begin to understand more and more of these words – they are content words, and they are important. ESL students will *never* understand every word that is spoken – but nobody does!

Besides, people love to talk about the weather, so the students will also be preparing to have real conversations with native speakers, which they are dying to do.

© Judy Thompson 2009

Sentences Student Page

Normal Conversation

English looks like this:

- What do you want to do?
- I don't know. What do you think?
- I don't know. Let's go out.
- Out where?
- I want to go to the mall.
- Shopping?
    - What do you want to buy?
- Nothing. I just want to look around.
- Well, I want to buy something.
- What do you want to buy?
- Ice cream.
- Sounds good.
- Let's go.

English sounds like this:

- Whadaya wanna do?
- I dunno. Whadaya think?
- I dunno. Let's go out.
- Out where?
- I wanna go ta tha mall.
- Shoppin?
    - Whadaya wanna buy?
- NuTHin. I jus wanna look around.
- Well, I wanna buy someTHin.
- Whadaya wanna buy?
- Ice cream.
- Sounds good.
- Lets go.

English has a **Nat**ural **Rhy**thm

The natural rhythm of English *speaking* is: ta DA da da DA da da DA

What do you want to do?	WHA da ya WANT ta DO?
I have to go to the store.	I HAVE ta GO ta tha STORE
I want to get some milk.	I WANna GET sa MILK
Do you want to come with me?	Da ya WANna COME with ME?

Don't expect to talk exactly like a native speaker, but understand that this is how people are talking to you. When you practice at home, get out your big elastic or clap your hands on every one of the bold green syllables. Your *speaking* will more closely resemble *native speaking*. Fun, eh?

www.thompsonlanguagecenter.com

Teacher Page   Sentences

Pausing

Written language is **solitary** and **timeless**. It can be read and reread at leisure.
Spoken language is **interactive** and **instantaneous**.

Conversation works because of pausing.

In **written** English, punctuation marks are a *system of inserting pauses in written matter* (which began in 1661) that separate elements and make the meaning clear.

In **spoken** English, there are many **pauses** because the listener needs **time** to **consider** what is being said to **formulate** a **response**.

Native speakers pause every three or four important words.

Did you ever notice when two people are having a conversation there is no hesitation between one person speaking and the other person answering? Too often, the second person doesn't even wait for the first person to finish speaking before they interrupt with their response. **Pausing** is the root of that phenomenon. There is enough **time,** in tiny **pauses,** when someone is speaking for the listener to **think**.

The **speed** at which humans **function**:	
Think	1,000 – 3,000 words per minute
Listen	150 – 250 words per minute
Speak	125 – 150 words per minute
Type	50 – 60 words per minute

Speaking is slower than listening, and much slower than thinking, so the listener can process what is being said. Think of phone numbers. Every few numbers there is a pause. No one can remember 5554519382 but they can remember 555 451 9382. If there is **no pausing**, the receiver doesn't have **time to process** and there is **no understanding**.

Student-to-Student Dictation

Adapt this style of paired *speaking* and listening exercise to the students' level.
- **Beginners** can practice **stress** and the difference between 13 and 30, 14 and 40…
- **Intermediate** students can practice saying big numbers.
- **Advanced** students practice ***pausing*** every three or four important words – as in reciting phone numbers.

If you are from **India**, you sound like a **runaway train** when you speak English.

Native English Speakers   can't   under   stand   this   style   of   speaking

You must PAUSE often.

© Judy Thompson 2009

Sentences   Student Page

Student-to-Student Dictation

Speaking **Pair Exercise**
Fold the paper down the center. Student A reads the numbers from the 1-15 on their page, and Student B writes what they hear in the blank spaces.
Halfway down the page, Student B reads and Student A writes.

Student 1		Student 2	
Say:		**Write:**	
Beginner		Beginner	
1	15	1	_____
2	50	2	_____
3	33	3	_____
4	14	4	_____
5	30	5	_____
Intermediate		Intermediate	
6	213-790-7900	6	___-___-____
7	907-624-8485	7	___-___-____
8	514-265-0025	8	___-___-____
9	706-438-9228	9	___-___-____
10	1 877-705-6536	10	_ ___-___-____
Advanced		Advanced	
11	102	11	_____
12	9,981	12	_____
13	7,080	13	_____
14	76,500	14	_____
15	328,495	15	_____
Write:		**Say:**	
Beginner		Beginner	
1	_____	1	16
2	_____	2	60
3	_____	3	73
4	_____	4	20
5	_____	5	13
Intermediate		Intermediate	
6	___-___-____	6	426-791-6868
7	___-___-____	7	503-341-4079
8	___-___-____	8	208-815-3451
9	___-___-____	9	917-284-2686
10	_ ___-___-____	10	1-800-447-4785
Advanced		Advanced	
11	___ ___ ___	11	890
12	___ ___ ___	12	1,481
13	___ ___ ___	13	3,052
14	___ ___ ___	14	67,370
15	___ ___ ___	15	145,809

Flip the page over and do the exercise again.

Sentences

Laundry List

Not All Words are Created Equally

What this means for the student is:

Important words are enough information

Stress important words. With the help of context and gestures, people will understand. Stop worrying about grammar.

1. Words are not all equally important.

2. There are important, less important, and unimportant words in *spoken* English.

3. Content words are important words for *speaking*.

4. Content words are:

    i. Nouns – person, place, thing
    ii. Verbs – action words
    iii. Adjectives – describe nouns
    iv. Adverbs – describe verbs
    v. Negatives – no, not, never...
    vi. Intensifiers – very, too, all...

5. All content words are always stressed (xxx.)

6. Less important words have a minor stress (xx.)

7. Unimportant words for *speaking* are called *function* or *grammar* words.

8. Function words are mostly important in *writing*.

9. Function words are:

    i. Articles – a, on, the
    ii. Conjunctions – and, but, or...
    iii. Verb *to be* – am, are, is...
    iv. Helping verbs – do, did, have, had...
    v. Modals – can, could, should, would, will
    vi. Pronouns – you, your, him, his
    vii. One-syllable prepositions – to, at, in, on...

10. Function words are not stressed (x.)

11. The vowel sound of function words (grammar words) is schwa – uh.

12. If necessary for meaning, any word can be stressed. This is called *focus*.

What Students Need to Know about Sentences

The thing about sentences is that, in *speaking*,
there aren't any.

- Native speakers run words together. People interrupt. They uh and ah… People start talking before the other person is finished speaking. They talk over top of each other and change the subject… Conversation is hard to follow.

- It is much easier for second language learners to communicate in English with each other than with native speakers because non-native speakers speak English more directly and plainly.

- *Speaking* is about transmitting ideas – important words will do the trick.

End of Part One

CONGRATULATIONS!

This book is about making people **aware** how native English speakers communicate. Awareness improves communication for everyone.

Part One is basic English – it will get students by in any circumstances.

Remember:
- Some words are important and some are not.
- Words that aren't important are not pronounced by native speakers, just grunted.
- Only listen to important words, which are pronounced clearly – higher, louder and longer than unimportant words.

The way to learn to speak English is by speaking it. Don't worry too much.

Before we leave the topic of content words, let's take a peek on page 132 at the other world of English – *writing* – and see what has been going on with content words there.

Stay tuned for Part Two.

Part Two develops advanced listening, *speaking* and communication skills.

Teacher Page　　　　　　　　　　Review of Part One

Review of Part One

Content Words Make History

In 1835, Samuel Morse invented the telegraph and made rapid long-distance communication possible. Urgent news traveled around the world faster and farther than ever before. Messages were short as the sender paid by the word. Telegrams delivered news of the first flight, the demise of the Titanic, world war and much more.

```
Kitty  Hawk N C Dec 17
Bishop M Wright
            7 Hawthorne St

Success four flights thursday  morning  all against twenty one mile
wind started from Level with engine power alone  average speed
through air thirty one miles longest 57 seconds inform  Press
home ~~####~~ Christmas .              Orevelle Wright     525P
```

In April 1912, a message from the North Atlantic to White Star Line read: "DEEPLY REGRET ADVISE YOUR TITANIC SUNK THIS MORNING FIFTEENTH AFTER COLLISION ICEBERG RESULTING SERIOUS LOSS LIFE FURTHER PARTICULARS LATER."

World history was told in content words:

```
From:   CINCPAC                        Date  7 DEC 41
To:     ALL SHIPS PRESENT AT HAWAIIN AREA.
Info:              = U R G E N T =
DEFERRED unless otherwise checked | ROUTINE | PRIORITY | AIRMAIL

AIRRAID ON PEARLHARBOR X THIS IS NO DRILL
```

Learners need to know that **content words** are **enough**.

Halifax Harbour, Nova Scotia, 1917

What do you think you're doing? shouted the chief clerk as train dispatcher Vince Coleman turned back towards the office. *We've only got a minute or two left! Anyone in the office won't stand a chance!* But Vince Coleman was thinking about the passenger trains speeding towards the threatened harbor. He had to stop them. In that moment of selfless action, Coleman telegraphed his urgent warning: STOP TRAINS. MUNITION SHIP ON FIRE. MAKING FOR PIER 6. GOODBYE.

At exactly 9:06 on December 6, 1917, the worst man-made explosion ever (before the atomic bomb on Hiroshima) tore through Halifax, claiming 2,000 lives, including the life of Vince Coleman.

But his message got through. Trains stopped all along the line. More than 300 lives were saved by two words: STOP TRAINS.

Full Circle

English communicates important information with content words.

In the past, there were telegrams: $/word

BABY GIRL 7 POUNDS 3:30 AM TUESDAY ALL WELL

Today, there are classified ads and public notice boards conveying **maximum information** with the **fewest symbols**:

> **Hartford-Main** 2 bdrm 1½ bath 4 appl's. A/C No pets $995/m cable incl. first/last 555-783-0570

> **Alton-Queen** 3bdrm 2 bath N/smkg fp. Lrg yard clean quiet amen avail imm. references $1,200/m + 282-669-3341

> **Weston-Mill** 1 bdrm bsmt apt. furn. appl's incl sep. ent. prkg $700/m incl util. 908-572-4991

Beginner Classified Exercise
1. How many bedrooms in the apartment at Alton and Queen Street?
2. Are pets allowed at the Hartford apartment?
3. Which location is a basement apartment?

Intermediate Classified Exercise
4. Which location has air conditioning?
5. Are furniture and appliances included with rent at Weston and Mill?
6. When is the Alton apartment available?

Advanced Classified Exercise
7. Which apartment is in a quiet neighborhood close to shopping?
8. Which apartment has a fireplace?
9. Is there a separate entrance or parking at Mill?

Teacher Page   Review of Part One

Same Old, Same Old

Texting: My smmr hols wr CWOT B4 we used 2go2 NY 2c my bro his GF+ 3 :- kids F2F. I LNY, it's a gr8 plc[7]

Translation: My summer holidays were a complete waste of time. Before, we used to go to New York to see my brother, his girlfriend and their three screaming kids face to face. I ♥ New York. It's a great place.

The lack of vowels in their alphabet did not matter to them because the nature of their language meant that an array of consonants was sufficient to give enough information to make clear what word was being written down, while occasional ambiguities would be handled by looking at the words in context.

A reference to the Phoenician alphabet in use in 700 B.C.

The Phoenician alphabet developed from Egyptian hieroglyphs (as did all alphabets), and our alphabet developed from the Phoenician one.

Phoenician **N** is a picture and a sound /n/.

It looks like an **owl** — it is an owl, but it also is an **M** and it makes the sound /m/.

Like the hieroglyphic and Semitic systems it evolved from, the Phoenician alphabet got by without using letters for vowels.

Answer Key

1. 3   **2.** no   **3.** Weston-Mill   **4.** Hartford   **5.** yes   **6.** immediately   **7.** Alton   **8.** Alton   **9.** yes

FYI (For Your Information): **Housing Ad Words and Abbreviations**

A/C	air conditioning	first/last	two months rent up front
apt	apartment	imm.	available immediately
appl's	appliances	incl.	included in the rent
amen	close to amenities	lrg	large
avail	available	N/	no
bath	bathroom	prkg	parking
bsmt	basement	sep. ent.	separate entrance
bdrm	bedroom	smkg	smoking
fp	fireplace	util.	utilities (hydro, water, phone)

---

[7] Written by a 13-year-old girl in Scotland.

© Judy Thompson 2009

Real Life English

Vanity License Plates

These are real license plates. Read them and match the words.

Beginner

4 GET IT	Be nice
CRZY 4U	I'm before you
B NICE	Forget it
THANX DAD	Potatoes
BIG BUX	Oh to be me
O2 BE ME	Crazy for you
IM B4 U	Thanks Dad
GR8 PL8	Tomatoes
POT8OS	Big bucks ($)
2OMATOZ	Great Plate

Intermediate – All these plates are a clue to the owner's occupation.

B KEEPR	Doc for Jocks – Orthopedic Doctor
DOC 4 JOX	Fly High – Pilot
DR IBALZ	Beekeeper – Apiary
FLY HI	Love to Teach – Teacher
4CASTR	Tennis Pro – Tennis Instructor
LV 2 TCH	Doctor Eyeballs – Optician
ITCH DR	Tooth Doctor – Dentist
NO P C ME	Forecaster – Meteorologist
STOX UP	Itch Doctor – Dermatologist
2TH DR	No Pee See Me – Urologist
10S PRO	Stocks Up – Stockbroker

Advanced – Some of these plates are single words and some are phrases.

XLER8	Late for a date
CALQL8	Excuse me
2 3PAIR	Not you again
NOT U AGN	Accelerate
L8 4 A D8	Six is enough (big family)
CU LAYTR	Little old lady
HV A GUD 1	Tooth repair
XUZ ME	For you to envy
6 IS ENUF	Calculate
4 U 2 NV	Love you for ever
LIL OLAD	See you later
LUV U 4 EVR	Have a good one (day)

The Future of *Writing*

Content words were the order of the day for rapid communication in the 1800s, and they are back at the top of the charts a hundred and fifty years later. From telegrams to text messaging, content words and simple clues get the job done.

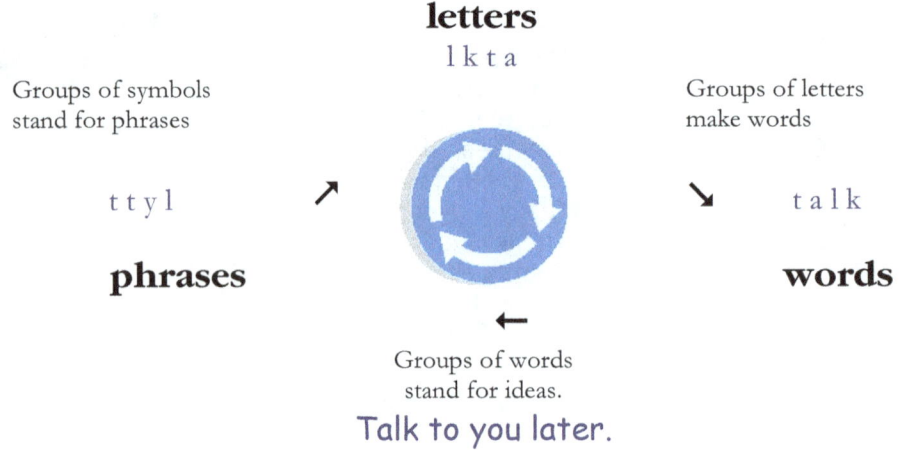

For the trials and tribulations of everyday life, native speakers often play with crazy English. It's fun.

For formal documents, scientific papers and business correspondence, the standard *written* English that is taught in school is still required.

(**l**augh **o**ut **l**oud/ **O**h **m**y **G**od or **g**osh/ **w**hat **t**he **f** word)

Part Two

ADVANCED

Linking

Expressions

Body Language

Chapter Four

LINKING

Words Don't Begin with Vowels

He mumbled his way to a fortune.
Sheb Wooley on Clint Eastwood

CHAPTER FOUR

Words Don't Begin with Vowels

Native speakers mumble. There is no mumbling in *writing*. Where does mumbling come from when native speakers talk? People mumble from:

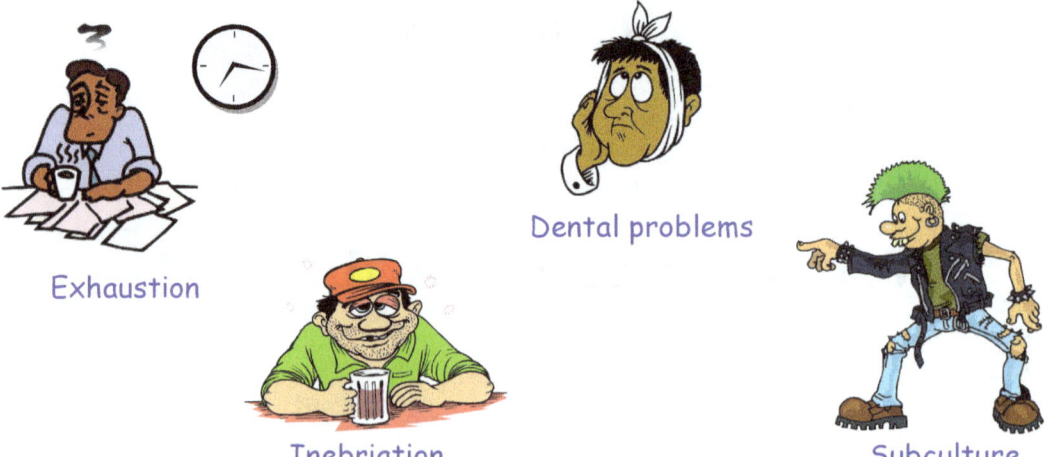

Exhaustion

Dental problems

Inebriation

Subculture

This is a trick question. Everyone mumbles in English – it's a part of the language. The **bad news** is that native speakers mumble so much, it is impossible for non-native speakers to understand them. The *good news* is that **mumbling is predictable**.

Mumbling is a mechanical part of *speaking* English and occurs with:

1. **Reduction,** which we talked about in Chapter Three, where unimportant syllables and words are reduced to uh and run together or disappear (whadaya).

2. **Linking** is about how English really sounds. In *speaking*, breaks between words don't occur exactly the way they look in print. Instead, people make sound breaks where it's **easiest**. Linking is the remixing and reinventing of sounds to make the process of *speaking* as physically easy as possible, regardless of spelling (wanna).

Talking the Talk

Human language is most easily articulated by alternating consonant and vowel sounds.

consonant · vowel · consonant · vowel … always beginning with consonants

It's a natural way for humans to produce speech. Although *written* English doesn't always follow the c · v · c · v model of language (e.g. **splash** – cccvcc), *spoken* English does because it's easier.

Students need to know:
People on the street are not going to speak to them in the word forms and vocabulary they have learned in school.

Mumbling

Native English speakers run words together when they speak. They mumble. Everybody does it – even presidents do. It's how English is *spoken*. It's not wrong or bad – it's just the way it is.

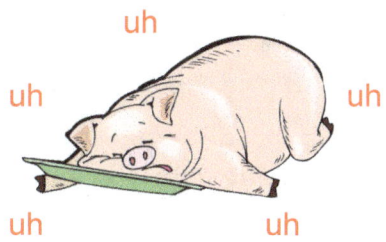

Fluent English speakers **grunt** a lot, which we already talked about. Unimportant words are grunted and *slurred* or *run together*.

and

Speakers are lazy. Mumbling is **easier** than *speaking* properly, which means *important* words can get slurred, too.

Luckily, there are predictable places where slurring happens. Native English speakers **don't pronounce two vowel sounds together,** and they **don't start words with vowel sounds.** They do something else – they **link**. Native English speakers link words together by sharing, stealing or adding sounds. They are not aware that they **constantly link words together**, so the process is rarely taught. When ESL students learn about **linking,** they understand native and fluent speakers better.

Rule #4   *Speaking* **flows independently of printed word breaks**.

Native speakers link words together where it's easiest to pronounce them. The sound of English doesn't line up with the printed words. That's another reason why no one learns to **speak** English by **reading** it.

It's an old chestnut but true:

You have to learn to **speak** English by **listening** to it.

Work out the *writing*, individual words and grammar later.

There is no other way to speak English than by **listening** to it, **practicing** it and **trusting** it will be okay in spite of mistakes.

www.thompsonlanguagecenter.com

Linking

Classroom Conversation

Student: Teacher, what means *noff*?
Teacher: There is no such word as *noff*. Where did you hear it?
Student: You.
Teacher: Me? What did I say?
Student: You say, "Tur *noff* your computers."
Teacher: Oops, you're right. I did say that. Sorry. Oh, look at the time! I'll have some more information about *noff* tomorrow.

You can guess that teacher was me. It was my introduction to **linking** (aka connected speech). Before that day, I didn't know what linking was, and I sure didn't know I was doing it. Now that I know about linking, I've never listened to English the same way since.

How did I get to be 45 years old, an ESL teacher and not know about linking? Because, humans learn to speak when they are very young. The process develops unconsciously. Children speak fluently before they reach school age and never need to study *how* to speak a first language.

Speaking English involves **linking**. Here's the scoop on linking:

- People speak in easy phrases, not crisp word units.
- *Speaking* flows independently of printed word breaks.
- Linking happens in **three predictable places**:
    1. Consonant · Consonant – the last sound in one word is the first sound in the next
    2. Consonant · Vowel – one word ends with a consonant, and the next word begins with a vowel
    3. Vowel · Vowel – one word ends with a vowel sound, and the next word begins with one
- Linking occurs inside sentences and phrases. Linking doesn't occur at the beginning of sentences, after commas or other punctuation.

Perfectly Good English

Linking explains a tremendous amount of what students can't find in the dictionary (like **noff**). Because of *linking* and *schwa*, **more than 85% of words heard in normal conversation** are not in the dictionary.

The ESL Student and the Dictionary

A standard dictionary is useless for learning to speak English because it's organized alphabetically and English is non-phonetic, and due to linking, most spoken word-clumps aren't in the dictionary. If dictionaries are for spelling, meaning and pronunciation, you can't look a word up unless you already know how to spell it. You must already have a sense of the meaning or how do you know it's the word you want to use, and IPA is a useless translation step away from the target language. **You can only use a dictionary if you don't need to.**

Standard dictionaries can be useful for writing, but not for speaking.
How do you say*? Is the only ESL dictionary for spoken English.*

Linking

Water flows downhill because it's easy.

Speaking flows like water – it takes the easiest route.

The **end** of one word **links**  to the **beginning** of the next by the **easiest** sound path. Words link in **three places:**

1. **C·C   Consonant to Consonant**
   The first consonant disappears.   goo**d d**og   /goo_ **d**og/

   When one word *ends* and the next word *begins* with the same consonant, the first consonant disappears.

   goo**d**   **d**og   goo_   **d**og

    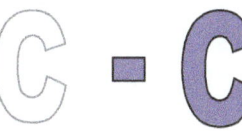 

2. **C·V   Consonant to Vowel**
   Words don't begin with vowel sounds.   tur**n o**ff   /tur_ **n**off/

   When a word *begins* with a vowel, *steal* the last consonant from the word before it.

   tur**n**   **o**ff   tur_   **n**off

3. **V·V   Vowel to Vowel**
   Vowel sounds can't be pronounced together.   **a e**gg   /a_**n**egg/

   When one word *ends* with a vowel sound and the next word *begins* with one, pronounce a consonant sound *in between*.

   a   **e**gg   a   **n**egg

Consonant to Consonant

Double consonants are usually pronounced as one*: ca<u>rr</u>ot – /ka rot/ (see pages 39 and 48). The same is true *between* words. When a word ends with the same consonant sound as the next word begins, the sound is only pronounced once.

Goo<u>d</u> <u>d</u>ay sounds like /goo <u>d</u>ay/.

I'm having a good day. /I'm havin' a goo day/.

(Australians go one step further and say G'day.)

Not in the Dictionary

This process is called **linking**, and it gives English thousands of familiar sounding words that can't be found in the dictionary (**dunno**.)

    Do<u>n</u>'t <u>k</u>now becomes donno *or* dunno.
        (The final **t** isn't pronounced; the **k** is silent – Chapter One.)

    I don't know. – I dunno.

ESL students try to speak English exactly as it is *written*. They *over* enunciate, and it NEVER WORKS. Native speakers are much lazier than that. Learners have accents from speaking **too carefully**. The accents don't matter for understanding, but the individuals are self-conscious. Knowing about **linking** can help them work out what is being said or, at the very least, students will stop expecting English to sound like it looks.

Perfectly Good English

Here is some familiar *spoken* English that is the result of reduction and linking.

Don't know – /duh NOW/	donno *or* dunno	I donno *or* dunno his name.
Want to – /WA nuh/	wanna	I wanna go home.
Going to – /GU nuh/	gonna	I'm gonna go home.
Have to – /HAF tuh/	hafta	I hafta go home for dinner.
Got to – /GO duh/	gotta	I gotta go. It's late.
Has to – /HAS tuh/	hasta	He hasta go home at 10.
Give me – /GI mEy/	gimme	Gimme a break.
Cup of – /CU puh/	cuppa	Gimme a cuppa coffee.

    S – Sure **s** will link with another **s**, but it'll link with anything if it becomes easier to say.
        This way – /thi_sway/
        Once more – /one_smore/

S is a bit sleazy.

She'll go home with anyone.

*Exceptions are cc and gg which can be two sounds i.e. accent and suggest.

Linking　　　　　　　　　　　　　　　　　　　　　　　　　　　Student Page

C·C

1. **C·C**　**Consonant to Consonant** – The first consonant disappears.

   Inside a word, double consonants are **pronounced** only **once** (page 49.)

ca**rr**ot	ba**ll**oons	ha**mm**er	e**gg**s
/ka rot/	/ba loonz/	/ha mer/	/egz/

NOT　car · rot　　bal · loonz　　ham · mer　　eg · gz

That doesn't sound right!

Between words, double consonant sounds are **pronounced** only **once** as well.

bla**ck c**offee	bu**s s**top	so**me m**ilk	oran**ge j**uice
/bla_koffee/	/bu_stop/	/su_milk/	/Oran_juice/

NOT　bla**k k**offee　　bu**s s**top　　su**m m**ilk　　oran**j j**uice

That doesn't sound right either!

Practice *Speaking* Like a Native

Intermediate – Read aloud.

big girl	take care	stop peeking
sad day	how wide	gain nothing
same month	fish shop	Mister Rogers
with thanks	eat toffee	call Laura

Advanced – Linking also happens with **sister sounds** (Chapter One, page 34)

hot dog	thank God	beige shoes
eat dinner	job posting	enough veggies
top banana	big kid	five fingers
please sit	with them	Rick's zipper

www.thompsonlanguagecenter.com　　　　145

Consonant to Vowel

Sentences can begin with vowel sounds – *I am funny* – but native English speakers begin all words inside of sentences with consonant sounds.

If a word in a sentence begins with a vowel sound and the word in front of it ends in a consonant sound, native speakers *steal* the consonant and move it to the next word. It's not weird that words don't start with vowels; it's weird that words aren't pronounced the way they are *written*!

Regardless of where printed words end in *written* English, *spoken* English internal words begin with consonant sounds.

Other Languages

Other languages begin words with consonants, then alternate consonants and vowels throughout because it's the easiest and most natural way to speak. Asian languages in particular stick closely to the easily pronounced C·V, C·V·C construction. *Written* English most definitely doesn't.

In the Cantonese and Vietnamese languages, words don't *end* in *consonants*. If I asked my husband how many were coming for dinner, he would say, Six for dinner, but if he were Cantonese he'd say, Si fo dinna.

The beauty of knowing how English is spoken is being able to specifically identify how other languages are different and then do something about it. When I tell Vietnamese students that English pronounces final consonants, they ask, Why didn' somebody tew me befo? And I say, I dunno.

Heartbreakers

Wonderful students try so hard to speak perfectly. They struggle to pronounce every letter, and it is heartbreaking because it doesn't help them sound like native speakers at all. English is a tricky, illogical, crazy language.

It's not through lack of effort that good students don't speak English.

Again, the best advice is to learn the language by listening to it, not reading it. There really is no shortcut or substitute for listening to hundreds of hours of English. If students aren't prepared to do that, then put the book down – no book will help them.

Answer Key

Intermediate:

big girl	bi_girl	take care	ta_care	stop peeking	sto_peeking
sad day	sa_day	how wide	ho_wide	gain nothing	gai_nothing
same month	sa_month	fish shop	fi shop	Mister Rogers	Miste_Rogers
with thanks	wi_thanks	eat toffee	ea_toffee	call Laura	ca_Laura

Advanced: sister sounds (page 34)

hot dog	ho_dog	thank God	than_God	beige shoes	bei_shoes
eat dinner	ea_dinner	job posting	jo_posting	enough veggies	enou_veggies
top banana	to_banana	big kid	bi_kid	five fingers	fi_fingers
please sit	plea_sit	with them	wi_them	Rick's zipper	Rick'_zipper

C·V

2. C·V Consonant to Vowel – Words inside sentences don't start with vowels. If a word starts with a vowel, steal the consonant before it.

Turn **o**ff the light.	tur_n**o**ff the light
turn **a**round	tur_n**a**round
night **i**n	nigh_d**i**n
far **a**cross	fa_r**a**cross
between **u**s	betwee_n**u**s
here **i**n	he_r**i**n
on **a**nd **o**n	o_n**a**n_d**o**n
touch **u**s	tou_ch**u**s
we'll **a**lways	we_l**a**lways

Rozi zare Red

Roses are red,	rozi_zare red
Violets are blue.	Vilet_sare blue
Sugar is sweet,	shuge_riz sweet
And so are you.	An so ware you

English looks like this: **Can I have a bit of egg?**

Find the **words** that **start** with **vowels.**

Can <u>I</u> have <u>a</u> bit <u>of</u> <u>egg</u>?

Underline the **link.**

Ca<u>n I</u> ha<u>ve a</u> bi<u>t of</u> <u>egg</u>?

l the **consonant sound,** and voila!

Ca_nI ha_va bi_da vegg?

Speak like a **native:**   ca nI ha va bi da vegg?

You know what to do. **Link** and **read** aloud:

North America	game over	global English
stop it	time out	native Indian
turn around	turn on	world economy
give it up	British Air	I'm unable

Teacher Page   Linking

Vowel to Vowel

Vowels are elastic sounds and can't be pronounced together. Go ahead and try to pronounce an **e** and an **i** together – you sound like you just woke up.

English contains hundreds of thousands of words beginning with vowels, but they are not pronounced the way they look. When a word ends with a vowel sound and the following word begins with a vowel sound, native speakers *throw in* an extra consonant sound *between* the vowels so they can physically produce speech.

When vowels occur between words, native speakers pronounce an invisible consonant – either a **w** or a **y** – to break up the run (see page 75). Students must learn to listen for consonants that aren't printed. For reference, check the Thompson Vowel Chart on page 55 in Chapter One. (/A<u>y</u>/, /E<u>y</u>/, /I<u>y</u>/, /O<u>w</u>/, /U<u>w</u>/…)

A or An?

That's why the article an comes before words beginning with a, e, i, o and u. Unfortunately, *written* English doesn't insert consonants routinely where they are found in *spoken* English. Native speakers don't know they do it, and ESL students aren't taught about the extra *invisible* sounds.

In Case They Ask

It's not necessary or empowering for students to study these exceptions, but a student may ask (there's one in every crowd.) Words that begin with vowels can follow the vowel sounds:

olive /o/   mustard /u/   or baby mustard /uh/ schwa.

The l<u>aw</u> <u>i</u>s to drive on the left.
The zebr<u>a</u> <u>e</u>ats grass.

Mercifully, there are few words in English that end in these vowel sounds, so exceptions are not a big deal.

**A regular dictionary is useless to people learning to speak English.
They can't find the words they hear.**

Answer Key 🗝

North <u>A</u>merica	Nor <u>th</u>america	game <u>o</u>ver	ga <u>m</u>over	global <u>E</u>nglish	globa <u>l</u>inglish
stop <u>i</u>t	sto <u>p</u>it	time <u>o</u>ut	ti <u>m</u>out	native <u>I</u>ndian	nati <u>v</u>indian
turn <u>a</u>round	tur <u>n</u>around	turn <u>o</u>n	tur <u>n</u>on	world <u>e</u>conomy	worl <u>d</u>economy
give <u>i</u>t up	gi <u>v</u>i dup	British <u>A</u>ir	Bridi <u>sh</u>air	I'm <u>u</u>nable	I <u>m</u>unable

© Judy Thompson 2009

V·V

3. **V·V** **Vowel to Vowel** – Two vowels together can't be pronounced.

Vowels are *elastic* sounds.

AAAAaaaaaaay   EEEEeeeeeeeey

Vowel sounds have to be **separated** by **consonants** to be **pronounced.**

That is why we need an **a** and an **a<u>n</u>**.

?   **a** <u>a</u>pple   **a** <u>e</u>lephant   **a** <u>i</u>ce cream cone   **a** <u>o</u>range   **a** <u>u</u>mbrella

I don't think so! The **n** in a**n** separates the vowel sounds from the vowel sound **a** for pronunciation.

a or an?

Chose the correct article in each blank space. *Hint: Read the words out loud.*

<u>an</u> A	__ I	__ Q	__ boy	__ unit
<u>a</u> B	__ J	__ R	__ egg	__ x-ray
__ C	__ L	__ S	__ window	__ echo
__ E	__ M	__ U	__ honor	__ unicorn
__ F	__ N	__ V	__ oven	__ woman
__ G	__ O	__ X	__ one-eyed man	__ university
__ H	__ P	__ Y	__ undershirt	__ European tour

Teacher Page   Linking

Ho Hum, This is Too Easy for Me

When the alphabet comes out, the advanced students get smug and think this exercise is too easy. And then they find they can't do it.

a/an Answer Key 🔑

an	A	an	I	a	Q	a boy	a unit
a	B	a	J	an	R	an egg	an x-ray
a	C	an	L	an	S	a window	an echo
an	E	an	M	a	U	an honor	a unicorn
an	F	an	N	a	V	an oven	a woman
a	G	an	O	an	X	a one-eyed man	a university
an	H	a	P	a	Y	an undershirt	a European tour

Lesson Idea

Students stumble in this simple exercise if they are still *reading* and not *listening* to the language.

a/an is a *sound* skill, not a spelling skill.

An honor – Since the **h** is silent, the first sound is a vowel sound.

It's about listening, not spelling.

The only listening most students do is in English class, to their teacher.
No student is going to live long enough to learn to speak English in class.
Encourage students to listen to and interact in English in the real world.

I Am

Vowel-to-vowel linking is not limited to a/an. There are hundreds of thousands of between-word, vowel-to-vowel combinations where one word ends in a vowel and the next word begins with one. The human mouth cannot easily produce back-to-back vowel sounds.

   I am /Iy/ /a/   What happens when they meet?

In *spoken* English, back-to-back vowel sounds are separated by the sound **w** or **y**.

Luckily, words that end in *vowels* usually end in *long vowels*.
Long vowels have their consonants built in!
   a /Ay/ gray   e /Ey/ green   i /Iy/ white
   o /Ow/ yellow   u /Uw/ blue

Other vowel sounds in final syllables are **Oy** as in **turquoise** and **Aw** as in **brown**. And look what is waiting at the end of them! **y** and **w** – perfect.
Er vowels already have the consonant **r** built in. Magic !☺

I YAM WHAT I YAM!

Popeye, the cartoon sailor, says.

© Judy Thompson 2009

V·V Continued...

Vowel to Vowel: Between words, there is an invisible **y** or **w**.

Writing   *Speaking*

I am   I **Y** am   I **y**am

he is   hE **Y** is   hE **y**iz

we are   WE **Y** are   wE **y**are

If any word ends with a vowel and the following word begins with a vowel, pronounce a '**w**' or a '**y**' consonant in between the two vowel sounds.

you are   you **w** are   you **w**are

go away   go **w** away   go **w**away

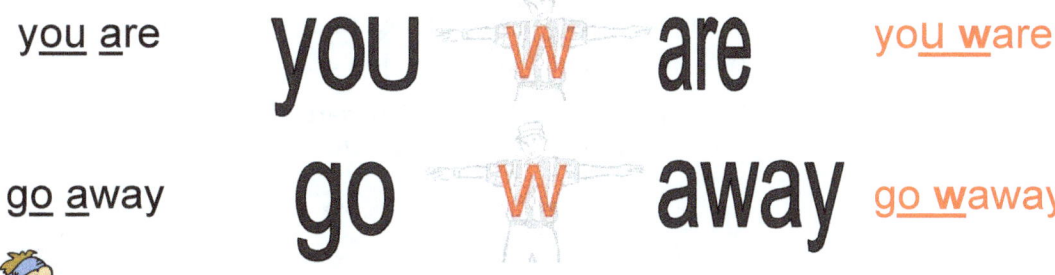

 When native speakers learn they insert consonant sounds unconsciously, they get all huffy and say,

No wIy don't!

Practice Native *Speaking*

the end the yend	Happy Easter	be on time
no answer	I often sing	so unusual
may I	dry ice	you open it
go on	video image	he isn't here
just do it	be able	do it after

Teacher Page　　　　　　　　　　Linking

🎵🎵 Juan and Don 🎵🎵

God bless Hollywood! Billions of people worldwide are familiar with the Titanic song. Help the students decode the sounds of the famous Titanic song with **FUSS**.

1. **F**ind the words that start with vowels.
2. **U**nderline the link.
3. **S**teal the consonant.
4. **S**ing/speak like a native.

For the first time, the English the students read will be the English they are familiar with. Students will ask for the song to be played over and over again. And they'll sing.

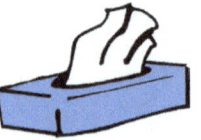

They might be so happy, they will buy you a coffee or a nice present.☺

Lesson Idea

Finding song lyrics is an entertaining and useful tool for students.

Type **l y r i c s** and the artist, title or a few words of a song and get the lyrics of songs from the internet. Using the FUSS method at home, students find lyrics on the internet and adjust the *linking* to represent exactly what they are hearing with any music they like. Linking lyrics is a fantastic way to support students in practicing at home.

HOT TIP for *Linking*: Look for internal words that start with vowels, steal a con-sonant, or add a y or a w – it's easier than you think.

Answer Key 🗝

the end	ThE yend	Happy Easter	HappE yeaster	be on time	bE yon time
no answer	nO wanswer	I often sing	I yofen sing	so unusual	sO wunusual
may I	mA yIy	dry ice	drI yice	you open it	yoU wope nit
go on	gO won	video image	vidEyO wimage	he isn't here	hE yisn't here
just do it	jus dU wit	be able	bE yable	do it after	dU wi dafter

ESL – English is a Secret Language

English is a *secret* language. It is no secret, native English speakers don't understand each other. For students, it's helpful to understand the disconnect between what they hear and the *written* English they studied about in school. Native speakers can't help because they are *not aware* of how English *speaking* is different from *writing*. They can only speak more slowly and loudly. The words natives speak are not found in any dictionary.

Students should know it's not them – it's English!

© Judy Thompson 2009

Linking　　　　　　　　　　　　　　　　　　Student Page

The Titanic Song

Find the words in the black column on the left that start with *vowels*, then fix the *linking*:

HOT TIP for *Linking*: Look for the whole words that start with vowels, steal a consonant, or add a **y** or a **w** – it's easier than you think.

My Heart Will Go Wo Nan Don

Every night **i**n my dreams	Every nigh **d**in my dreams
I see you **I** feel you.	I see you **wI** feel you
That **i**s how **I** know you go **o**n.	Tha **d**is ho **wI** know you go **wo**n
Far **a**cross the distance	Fa **r**across the distance
And spaces between **u**s	And spaces betwee **nu**s
You have come to show you go **o**n.	You have come to show you go **wo**n
Near, far, wherever you **a**re	Near, far, wherever you **wa**re
I believe that the heart does go **o**n.	I believe that the hear**t d**oes go **wo**n
Once more you **o**pen the door	On**ce m**ore you **wo**pen the door
And you're here **i**n my heart	And you're he **ri**n my heart
And my heart will go **o**n **a**nd **o**n.	And my heart will go **wo** **n**an **d**on
Love can touch **u**s **o**ne time	Love can tu **ch**us**wo**ne time
And last for **a** lifetime	And last fo **ra** lifetime
And never let go till we're gone.	And never let go till we're gone
Love was when **I** loved you	Love was whe **nI** loved you
One true time **I** hold to	One true ti **mI** hold to
In my life we'll **a**lways go **o**n.	In my life we **la**lways go **wo**n
Near, far, wherever you **a**re	Near, far, wherever you **wa**re
I believe that the heart does go **o**n.	I believe that the hear**t d**oes go **wo**n
Once more you **o**pen the door	On**ce m**ore you **wo**pen the door
And you're here **i**n my heart	And you're he **ri**n my heart
And my heart will go **o**n **a**nd **o**n.	And my heart will go **wo** **n**an **d**on
You're here, there's nothing **I** fear,	You're here, there's nothin **gI** fear
And **I** know that my heart will go **o**n.	An **dI** know that my heart will go **wo**n
We'll stay forever this way	We'll stay forever thi**s** **w**ay
You **a**re safe **i**n my heart	You **wa**re sa **fi**n my heart
And my heart will go **o**n **a**nd **o**n.	And my heart will go **wo** **n**an **d**on

Answers in **red** on the **right**.

Music: James Horner; Lyrics: Will Jennings; Performed by Celine Dion in the movie Titanic (1997).

www.thompsonlanguagecenter.com

At a Restaurant

The waiter asks the couple if they would like soup 'r salad with their meal.

Soup or salad?

She is happy with her soup.

Super salad?

He is disappointed – he doesn't think his salad is that *super*.

English is not clear. Between reduced vowels and linking, native speakers rely heavily on *guessing* to understand what is being said. When they aren't sure, they say, Pardon?

From This Day Forward

One evening, impressed by a meat entrée my wife had prepared, I asked, "What did **you marinate this in**?" She dropped her fork and went into a long explanation about how much she loves me and how life wouldn't be the same without me. I must have looked confused by her response, because she inquired, "Well, what did you ask me?"

When I told her, she laughed and said, "I thought you asked if I would **marry you again**!"

Later I asked her, "Hey, Hon, would you marry me again?" Without hesitation, she replied, "Vinegar and barbecue sauce."

Roger Welsch
Readers Digest Excerpt from February 2008

WHuh duh yuh

Sentence Surgery

Cut up the little phrase **WHuh duh yuh** to see **why** it's **crazy**, so we never have to do it again.

What do you want?

Wha		unstressed – Whuh
t do	t and d – C · C linking	unstressed – duh
you		unstressed – yuh

⎫ WHuhduhyuh **WANT**?

Sometimes *written*: **Whadaya want?**

What are you doing?

Wha		unstressed – Whuh
t are	C · V linking – /t/ between vowels is /d/	unstressed – duh
you		unstressed – yuh

⎫ WHuhduhyuh **DOin'**?

Sometimes *written*: **Whadaya doin'?**

Because of *schwa* and *linking*, **What Do You…** and **What Are You…** sound exactly the same – **Whadaya**.

Perfectly Good English

Many perfectly good *spoken* English words are not found in the dictionary. **Guess** what these spoken phrases are and write them out in the blank spaces on the right.

1. Whadayawanna do? __ __ __ __ __ __ __ ?
2. Jagecher hair cut? __ __ __ __ __ __ __ ?
3. CanI hava bida veg? __ __ __ __ __ ?
4. My heart will go wonandon. __ __ __ __ __ __ .
5. Someday, love's gonna getcha. _____, ____ __ _____.
6. Gimme a break. __ __ __ __ .
7. Gimme a cuppa tea. __ __ __ __ __ .
8. Jafta go now. __ __ __ __ ?
9. Jawanna geda cuppa coffee? __ __ __ __ __ __ ?
10. Mayapoose next please? __ __ __ __ __ ?

A Short Glossary of Perfectly Good English

CUPPA – cup of
DUNNO – don't know
GETCHA – get you
GONNA – going to (future)
GOTTA – got to (must)
JAFTA – Do you have to?
JAGECHER – Did you get your…
JAWANNA – Do you want to…
JEETYET – Did you eat yet?
LOTSA – lots of

MAYAPOOSE – May I help who is
SALOTTA – is a lot of
SUPERSALAD – soup or salad, or super salad
WHADAYA – What do you…, or What are you…
WANNA – want to
WHADDUP – What is up (slang greeting)
SNUF – is enough (that's enough)
NOFF – …n off
W^JA / DIJA – would you / did you
YASHUDA – you should have

More Real English

Shania Twain is a music star who prints out some of her lyrics exactly the way they sound! Here are a few lines from her *Up* album. Music makes fantastic fill-in-the-blank listening exercises. Have your students write out the underlined words. Enjoy Shania!

I'm Gonna Getcha Good!

Don't <u>wantcha</u> for the weekend, don't <u>wantcha</u> for a night
I'm only interested if I can have you for life, yeah
Uh, I know I sound serious and baby I am
You're a fine piece of real estate, and I'm <u>gonna</u> get me some land

(I'm <u>gonna</u> <u>getcha</u>)
I'm <u>gonna</u> <u>getcha</u> while I <u>gotcha</u> in sight
(I'm <u>gonna</u> <u>getcha</u>)
I'm <u>gonna</u> <u>getcha</u> if it takes all night
(Yeah, you can <u>betcha</u>)
You can <u>betcha</u> by the time I say go, you'll never say no

Answer Key

1. Wadayawanna do?
2. Jagecher hair cut?
3. CanI havabida veg?
4. My heart will go wonandon
5. Love's gonna getcha.
6. Mayonais alotta people here.
7. Ya didn't bring the kids wijadija?
8. Jafta go now?
9. Wanna geda cupa coffee?
10. Mayapoose next please?

What <u>do</u> <u>you</u> <u>want</u> <u>to</u> do?
Did <u>you</u> get <u>your</u> hair cut?
Can <u>I</u> have <u>a</u> bit <u>of</u> egg?
<u>My</u> heart <u>will</u> go <u>on</u> and <u>on</u>.
Love <u>is</u> going <u>to</u> get <u>you</u>.
Man there <u>is</u> <u>a</u> lot <u>of</u> people <u>here</u>.
<u>You</u> didn't bring <u>the</u> kids <u>with</u> <u>you</u>, did <u>you</u>?
<u>Do</u> <u>you</u> have <u>to</u> go now?
<u>Do</u> <u>you</u> want <u>to</u> get <u>a</u> cup <u>of</u> coffee?
<u>May</u> <u>I</u> help whose next please?

Linking Student Page

Perfectly Good English
Spoken Word Search Puzzle

- There are 24 common *speaking* phrases hidden in the puzzle.
- Find the phrases and circle them.
- Phrases can be printed forward, backward, up, down or on the diagonal.

Yabut! Yabut, they aren't in the dictionary! It's still English – it's *spoken* English.

```
Z Z W Y U D B Y K Y W Y J Z A R A L B K
B E I O A P E A J A J A W Y F C H O E K
J Z J G D S T O N A W A A D S B C T T K
F J A P A O H N N A G D F O E E T S C W
Z C D M L T A U N N A E J T S C N A H H
V Q I Z A R A N D H O X C O A W A Z A V
G A J N S O A T W A G D O H I Z W W J I
Z W A N R M B J T D T P F E E F F O N C
T E Y T E E J T G O A T V X I R C W O H
F Q C P P D O E H Y L S W H A D D U P A
H U V P U G T F A A M A I H H G I L Q N
G T N H S C U M P J Q K S B G I Q S P N
S G S S H A E X V T A O P K L E W Y O
R G H A F T A P P U C C O U L D J E R G
```

BETCHA	…I bet you…	LOTSA	…lots of…
COULDJER	…could your…	MAYAPOOSE	May I help who's…?
CUPPA	…cup of…	NOFF	…n off
DONNO	…don't know…	SALOTTA	That is a lot of…
GETCHA	…get you…	SNUF	That is enough.
GONNA	…going to… (future)	SUPERSALAD	…super salad / soup or salad
GOTTA	…got to… (must)	WANNA	…want to…
HAFTA	…have to… (must)	WANTCHA	…want you…
JAFTA	Do you have to?	WHADAYA	What do you…/What are you …?
JAGECHER	Did you get your…?	WHADDUP	What is up?
JAWANNA	Do you want to?	W^JA DIJA	would you / did you…
JEETYET	Did you eat yet?	YASHUDA	You should have…

www.thompsonlanguagecenter.com   157

Teacher Page   Linking

Say What?

When native speakers aren't sure what is being said (which is often), they **guess**. Sometimes when native speakers guess, they come up with an idea or phrase that makes sense even though the guess is wrong – it's different from the original message. These **wrong guesses** have a special name – **mondegreens.** A **mondegreen** is phrase that is **misheard** in such a way that it acquires a new meaning.

mondegreen (MON duh green) – noun

The word **mondegreen** is itself a mondegreen. American writer Sylvia Wright coined the term in her essay ***The Death of Lady Mondegreen*** about an anonymous seventeenth-century Scottish folk song that was read to her. She writes:

When I was a child, my mother used to read aloud to me from *Percy's Reliques*. One of my favorite poems began, as I remember:

They have slain the **Earl Amurray**   And **Lady Mondegreen**

What was actually printed was:

They have slain the Earl of Moray   And laid him on the green

Ever since, *mishearings* have been called *mondegreens* in honor of Lady Mondegreen.

Perfectly Good English 🗝

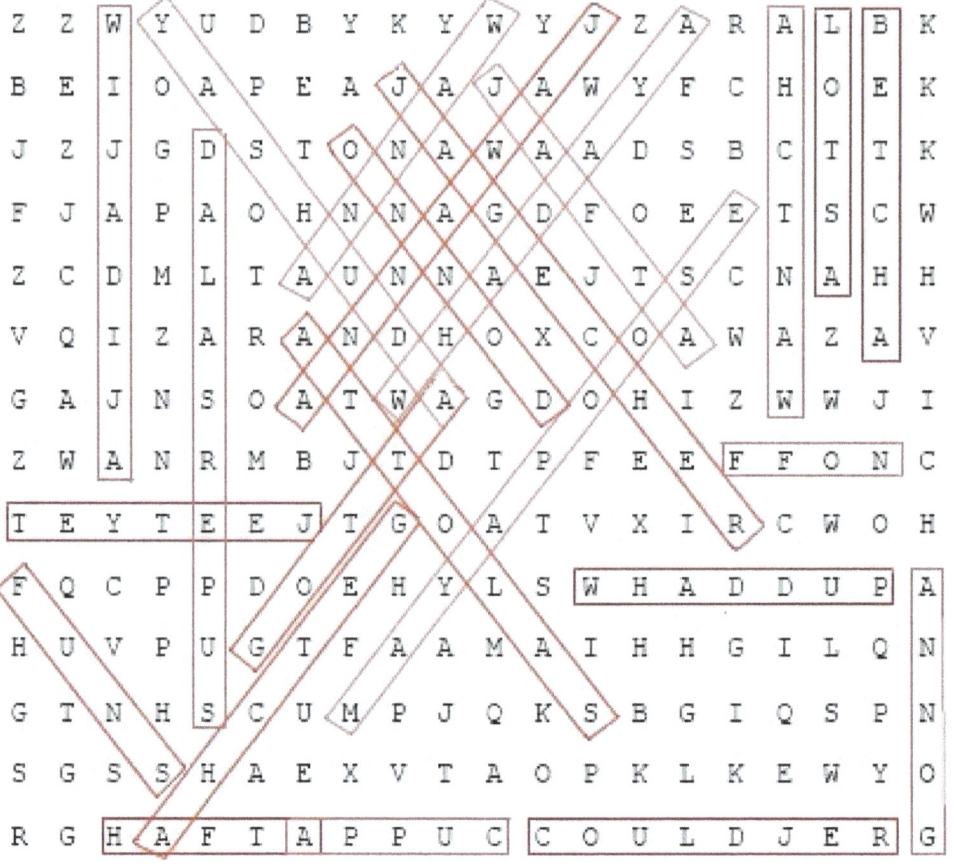

© Judy Thompson 2009   158

Fun with English

Kids like the comic character *Bart Simpson* have fun with *linking* when they make a phone call and ask to speak to **Seymour Butts** or **Amanda Hugginkiss**, knowing when the names are repeated, they will sound like **see more butts** and **a man to hug and kiss**.

It's funny!

Native speakers know that English is ridiculous. Sometimes you just have to laugh. When native speakers mishear what is being said, they guess and make something up!

Children learn their national anthem before they can read. From listening to it, some kids believe the words to the Star-Spangled Banner go like this:

Jose, can you see by the dawnzer lee light
What so proudly we hailed at the twilight's glass cleaner…

When they learn the real words, they can't believe it! It's funny!

For all intents and purposes	For all intensive purposes
A blessing in disguise	A blessing in the skies
Spitting image	Spit and image

Guessing and making things up to fit words poorly heard is very common and has a special name – **mondegreen**. Mondegreen is something all native speakers have experienced, even if they don't know what it's called. Knowing the name is interesting – but it's not important, like *subordinate clause* or *phrasal verb*.

For fun around the campfire, kids will have their friends repeat nonsense phrases like: owha tagoo siyam until they undo the linking and hear it differently – Oh what a goose I am.

It's funny!

www.thompsonlanguagecenter.com

Teacher Page   Linking

Who Cares?

Technical information can be interesting, but beyond a certain point, it is counterproductive. That's why grammar-based learning never results in successful *speaking*. More information does not empower learners – it confuses them. More information = better speaker? Not at all! When is enough grammar enough?

Right Now

An effective method for learning a new language is the monkey method – **monkey see**, **monkey do**. In this case, it's monkey hear, monkey say. Learners simply mimic what they hear – **before they understand the words.** It is a powerful learning tool. (They do this not to someone's face obviously, but in their own homes, in front of the TV… soap operas, talk shows, YouTube, podcasts, Facebook, reels…)

Success Story

International TV personality Ismael Cala always wanted to be a television broadcaster. He became a TV broadcaster in his native Cuba and still wanted to be one when he immigrated to Canada, but he didn't speak English. He watched *Oprah* every day and **repeated** everything she said. For three months, he didn't know what she was saying or understand what he was repeating. After three months, however, he suddenly began to understand English. When he began to speak English, he was perfectly intelligible. He **sounded** like a North American – with a charming Spanish accent.

This man was willing to do what few adults will choose to do. He was willing to **suffer**, continuing to listen to English for months and months without understanding what anyone was saying. **He learned the language by listening and mimicking**.

Now he works at his dream job as an anchor for a major television news station.

Stephanie Wei, *Today's Canadian*, September 2005

What Students Need to Know about *Linking*

Relax. It's everywhere and no one can do anything about it. Don't even try to translate the mumbling. After students have listened to enough English, one day they will wake up and understand what people are saying.

The real homework is **suffering** and **trusting** – choosing to be immersed in English when they don't know what people are saying.

When they have **heard** enough (about 300-500 hours), they will start to understand.

> *The finest language is mostly made up of simple unimposing words.*
> George Eliot

To the students, this means: Native speakers don't start words with vowels.

© Judy Thompson 2009

Laundry List

Chapter Four
Linking

1. Mumbling is normal when *speaking* English.

2. Mumbling is the result of reduction and **linking** (also know as connected speech).

3. Linking makes it physically easier for people to speak.

4. The easiest way for humans to speak is by alternating consonant and vowel sounds, beginning with consonant sounds (C·V or C·V·C patterns).

5. Linking is the term for the shift in *speaking* breaks independent of printed word units.

6. Linking **happens predictably in three common situations:**

    C·C – When a word ends with the same or similar consonant sound that the next word begins with, you only pronounce the sound once (**goo_dog**).

    C·V – When a word ends with a consonant sound and the following word begins with a vowel sound, steal the consonant from the end of the first word and pronounce it as the beginning of the second word (**tur_noff** the light).

    V·V – When a word ends with a vowel sound and the following word begins with a vowel sound, insert an *invisible* **w** or **y** (see page 75) (**go waway**).

7. Linking does not occur through any punctuation marks.

8. Linking happens inside phrases. It doesn't start sentences.

Chapter Five

Expressions

Words Come in Groups

A short saying often contains much wisdom.
Sophocles

Teacher Page   Expressions

CHAPTER FIVE

Words Come in Groups

Context

English words don't make sense on their own. The surrounding text, conversation or situation provides **context** and lets us know what individual words mean. In a romantic restaurant, **love** is a **feeling**. In a conversation about tennis, **love** is a **score**. In English, words come in small groups and work together to produce mental images. **Context** is critical to understanding individual words, phrases or conversations.

When native speakers hear or read new vocabulary, they have only one question:

What does _____ mean?

And the response is always the same –

What is the sentence?

whirled peas

world peace

Student: What means **whirled peas**?
Teacher: **What's the sentence**?
Student: We prayed for **whirled peas**.

Reading / *Speaking* / Guessing

Reading vocabulary is much larger than *speaking* vocabulary. **Reading is solitary,** and the reader can review text and think about new words *in context*.

Speaking **or conversation is fleeting** and spontaneous. There is no time to think about new words. *Speaking* uses a much smaller vocabulary than *writing*.

Whether *spoken* or *written*, native speakers **guess** the meaning of words from their **context**. In the bride example on the opposite page, one can instantly guess the meaning of made-up words. From the context, we know that *mullings* are some kind of decoration and *saftlets* must be flowers.

Native speakers develop abstract language skills in grade school by *playing* with context.

Why should you never marry a tennis player?

Because love means nothing to them.

Out of Context!

When information or quotations have been repeated in part and without giving the circumstances, they have been *taken out of context*. It's why you can't trust social media or the news which are selected bits of information that serve an agenda.

© Judy Thompson 2009

Words Come in Groups

Words are *units* of language,

but words don't stand on their own.

The **context** is the surrounding **words** and **situation**.
Context **tells us** what an individual word **means**.

Love can be a **verb**.  *Love* can be a **noun**.
I *love* you. Love is grand.

Love can be an **adjective**.
A *love* letter.

Love can be a **proper noun**.
I'd like you to meet Dr. John *Love*.

Love can be an **informal address**.
Be a *love* and pour me a cuppa tea.

 *Love* can be a **tennis score** and it means zero.
She won the first set six-*love*.

Rule #5 **Words work together in groups.**

Context is so powerful that you can *figure out* the meaning of new words from their context, even if they are made-up words like *mullings* and *saftlets* below:

The bride wore a long white gown trimmed with lace and swirls of pearl *mullings*. In her hand, she carried a bouquet of tiny pink *saftlets*.

Teacher Page   Expressions

Make Up

Make up is a **noun** when she's putting it on her face.

Make up is a **verb** when people have finished a disagreement.

The situation provides the meaning of the words and a little bit more…

Anticipation

Situations are context for words people *expect* to hear. Given the situation, people *anticipate* what is going to be said. When someone speaks to them, they only half-listen – mostly to confirm, *That's what I thought he was going to say.* Native speakers don't listen to what is actually being said. In new situations, at school, jobs or volunteering, native speakers have to listen **very hard** to instructions, and others have to **show** them what to do because language is not enough information. When situations and routines become familiar, they provide **context** for natural, flowing communication.

Basic English

One word – one meaning. In 1930, David Ogden developed a basic list of 850 words with no double meanings and a simplified grammar system with only ten rules. It was the first step in developing a simplified version of English that has since been taught around the world. The simplified English that is now understood by 2 billion people worldwide is known as ***International English.*** There are no expressions in ***International English***. Ironically, in international meetings today, it's the native speaker who can't be understood because of their excessive use of words and phrases with double meanings and idiomatic expressions.

Context Exercise

Choose the word that fits best in the sentence.

Beginner

1. It's (two, to, too) cold.
2. She (ate, eight) too much pasta.
3. Ouch! I got something in my (I, eye).
4. The rent is two months past (dew, do, due).
5. He asked for another (peace, piece) of pie.
6. I don't (know, no) what you are talking about.
7. Mrs. Johnson couldn't (cell, sell) her home.
8. The old guy can't (hear, here) what you are saying.
9. My (aunt, ant) is very attractive. She looks like Julia Roberts.
10. How many (four, for, fore) dinner?

Intermediate

11. My husband eats (cereal, serial) every morning for breakfast.
12. I love the (cent, scent, sent) of that candle.
13. It was love at first (cite, sight, site).
14. She froze like a (dear, deer) in the headlights.
15. That no-smoking (ad, add) was very effective.
16. The (capital, capitol) of Italy is Rome.
17. The store will (altar, alter) my pants for free.
18. To (err, heir, air,) is human.
19. He had a beautiful (base, bass) guitar.
20. Give me the (bear, bare) facts.

Advanced

Choose the word or phrase that fits best and read the sentences out loud.

21. (Their, they're, there) is no place like home.
22. The bandage was wound around the wound.
23. He took a shot and the dove dove into the bushes.
24. The insurance was invalid for the invalid.
25. It's the (cross-eyed bear, cross I'd bear).
26. After a number of injections, my jaw got number.
27. I live next to the stadium where bands play live.
28. The buck does funny things when the does are present.
29. The clothes were too close to the closet door to close it.
30. Don't wait! There is no time like the present to present a present.

Teacher Page   Expressions

Collocations

Half the truth is the same as a lie.
ESL students have been taught half the truth.

Adjectives describe nouns.
Adverbs describe verbs…
If these grammar rules were strictly true, then
Merry New Year, Happy Christmas and Merry Birthday
would be English – **but they aren't.**

The truth is, some adjectives describe some nouns – sometimes. When two or more words occur together and they have a special bond, they are called *collocations*. English is composed of hundreds of thousands of these tiny groups of words that native speakers use unconsciously, simply because they *sound right*.

Teachers truly believe that grammar is the basis of English. This is what they were taught. **But it isn't so.** Never mind – that is the past. The important thing now is to move forward. One of the most empowering things students will ever learn is that English is made up of collocations, not grammar.

Happy New Year, **Merry Christmas** and **Happy Birthday** are **collocations**. They are special little groups of words that come together **for no rational reason.**

The words and the order are fixed.

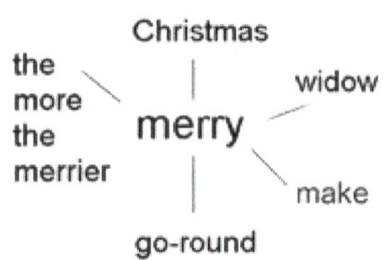

Word diagrams may help students.

There are **few** words that go naturally with **merry**:
merry-go-round, merry widow, make merry,
the more the merrier. That's it.

There is no such thing as **merry car** or **merry snow**, even though **car** and **snow** are nouns and **merry** is an adjective.

- **Collocations are how English is really put together,** not grammar.
- Collocations are small fixed groups of words that come together **for no reason** to convey images.

Answer Key

Beginner	**Intermediate**	**Advanced**
1. **too** cold	11. eats **cereal**	21. There's no place like home
2. She **ate**	12. **scent**	22. wound around the wound. /wʌwnd/, /wuwnd/
3. my **eye**	13. love at first **sight**	23. dove dove into the bushes. /duv/, /dowv/
4. past **due**	14. like a **deer**	24. invalid for the invalid. /in VA lid/, /IN va lid/
5. **piece** of pie	15. **ad**	25. It's the cross I'd bear.
6. I don't **know**	16. **capital** of Italy	26. number of injections… number. /numbEr/, /numEr/
7. **sell** her home	17. **alter** my pants	27. I live next to the stadium… play live. /liv/, /lIyv/
8. can't **hear**	18. To **err**	28. does funny … does are present. /duz/, /dowz/
9. My **aunt**	19. **bass** guitar	29. clothes … close … to close it. /klowz/, /klows/, /klowz/
10. **for** dinner	20. **bare** facts	30. present, to present a present. /PRE sent/, /pre SENT/, /PRE sent/

© Judy Thompson 2009

The Most Important Page in the Book

Collocation

English is not about grammar at all.

You have been misled.

The truth is,
some adjectives describe
some nouns, and
there is **no logic** to it.

Words come in *special little groups* called *collocations*.

For example:
- *merry* and *happy* are **adjectives**, so they describe nouns.
- *merry* and *happy* are also **synonyms**, so they mean the same thing.

but you can't say:

<u>Merry</u> New Year!   <u>Happy</u> Christmas!   <u>Merry</u> Birthday

These are not English.

Black and white means clarity (or an old TV set.)
   There it is in black and white.

White and black has no special meaning.
   The dog is white and black.

A **pretty girl** is beautiful; a **pretty boy** can mean homosexual.

Over<u>look</u> is not the same but the opposite of **over<u>see</u>**.

Random Word Pairings

Words **collocate** when they go **naturally together** like **spare time**, **get married** and **blue moon**. There is no reason for these random groupings. They are everywhere. When a student learns English from *grammar*, they write perfect paragraphs like this.

Last night, I cooked chicken for my family. We ate dinner at 7:00, then my husband washed the dishes. After dinner, we drank coffee and watched TV.

Absolutely perfect, no mistakes, A+.
It's not wrong, but native speakers **don't** say it like that. They say it like this:

Last night, I <u>made</u> chicken for my family. We <u>had</u> dinner at 7:00, then my husband <u>did</u> the dishes. After dinner, we <u>had</u> coffee in front of the TV.

Wikipedia on Collocations

Knowledge of collocations is vital for the competent use of a language: a grammatically correct sentence will stand out as awkward if collocational preferences are violated.

If there are no **rules** for collocations and studying grammar isn't the answer, how are students supposed to learn English? This is a recording – **from LISTENING TO ENGLISH.**

Don't be discouraged. Students remember more than they think they do, and if they have been listening to English, they will begin to recognize what *sounds right* fairly quickly once they are trained to listen for **high notes** and **groups of words**.

If students aren't listening to English, no one can help them. They actually have to do that work themselves. It's outside the classroom, and it's hundreds of hours of listening to English before recognizing words that go together.

Make · Do · Have · Get Exercise

Examples:
Married collocates only with get – you can get married. Married does not collocate with make, do, or have. You cannot make married, do married or have married.
Lunch collocates with make, do, have and get, each with different meanings.
- Make lunch is **prepare** it.
- Do lunch is **meet and eat** – probably at a restaurant.
- Have lunch is **eat** it.
- Get lunch is to **procure** in some way, but it also means **now** or **soon**.

Expressions   Student Page

Make · Do · Have · Get

Put a check mark ✓ under each verb that goes with the noun in the first column.

Go ahead – say them out loud: *make married, do married, have married* and *get married.* Which one is right?

Make married? – sounds ridiculous!

	make	do	have	get
Example: married				✓
1. lunch				
2. love				
3. homework				
4. dishes				
5. going				
6. a mistake				
7. money				
8. laundry				
9. a haircut				
10. fun				
11. lost				
12. sick				
13. friends				
14. dinner				
15. a headache				
16. a job				
17. ready				
18. jokes				

You know more than you think!

Pay attention to words in their groups because that's how English speakers use them – not individually.

www.thompsonlanguagecenter.com

Teacher Page   Expressions

Collocations are Fixed

House and *home* are synonymous but,

house work
is not the same as **home work**.

Overhang is not the same as
hang over.

Up Your Nose

The same word has a slightly different *sense* in every collocation.

UP for example: It's easy to understand UP, meaning toward the sky or at the top of the list, but when we awaken in the morning, why do we wake UP? At a meeting, a topic comes UP? We speak UP or shut UP, and it is UP to the secretary to write UP a report. Officers are UP for election. We call UP our friends; we brighten UP a room, polish UP the silver; we warm UP the leftovers and clean UP the kitchen. We lock UP the house, and some guys fix UP old cars. This is only the *tip of the iceberg* for UP. People stir UP trouble, line UP for tickets, work UP an appetite, and think UP excuses. To be dressed is one thing, but to be dressed UP is special. For more information, look it UP in the dictionary.

Answer Key

	make	do	have	get
1. lunch	prepare	meet and eat	eat	obtain now
2. love	sex			feel
3. homework		study	assigned	in future
4. dishes	gourmet	wash	own	procure
5. going				hurry
6. a mistake	error		pregnant, no father	
7. money	earn		rich	ATM
8. laundry		wash	need to wash	
9. a haircut			haircut done	haircut required
10. fun	tease		enjoy yourself	
11. lost				go away
12. sick	disgust			become ill
13. friends	connect		popular	invite
14. dinner	cook		eat	buy
15. a headache			in pain	increasing
16. a job		work	employed	job search
17. ready				prepare
18. jokes	tell			understand

© Judy Thompson 2009

Look, Watch, See

Fill in the blanks with <u>a form of</u> **look**, **watch** or **see** to complete the sentences.

Example: Do you _____ what I mean?

Do you _see_ what I mean?

1. Take a _____ at this.
2. What are you _____ on TV?
3. You _____ like a million bucks.
4. I _____ an opportunity and I went for it.
5. What are you _____ at?
6. He _____ angry.
7. Can you _____ the kids while I go to the store?
8. On Friday nights we like to _____ movies at home.
9. Ornithology is bird _____.
10. My aunt raises _____ - eye dogs for the blind.
11. It _____ like it's going to rain.
12. Are you _____ anyone or would you like to go for coffee?
13. He should _____ his money more closely.
14. I can _____ for miles from here.
15. _____ me up when you are in town.
16. My _____ is broken. Do you have the time?
17. He over _____ the details.
18. She over _____ the whole operation.
19. _____ me Mom!
20. _____ at the mess you made!
21. Have you been _____ the news?
22. _____ your head!
23. If you _____ to your left you will _____ the river.
24. The police are _____ him.
25. Do you _____ the difference?

English is Abstract

We know what **fall** means, we know what **in** means, and we know what **love** means. Put them all together and you get *fall in love,* which is a much bigger picture or image than the individual little words suggest by themselves. ***Fall in love*** is an abstract image.

 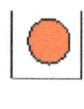  

fall   in   love

Really good ESL students write paragraphs like this:

 When the young man and woman met, they looked into each other's eyes for a long time. They had warm feelings inside, and they decided to spend a lot of time together.

There is not much to correct in that effort, but an English speaker would never say any of it. A native speaker would say:

They fell in love.

English is made of thousands of little word groups or expressions that suggest images or mental pictures. Students use grammar to explain everything because they don't know the expression!

The expression a native English speaker would use about expressions is:

The whole is greater than the sum of the parts.

It's a strange world of language in which skating on thin ice can get you into hot water.   Franklin P. Jones

Look, Watch, See Answer Key

1. look	9. watching	17. looked
2. watching	10. seeing	18. seeing
3. look	11. looks	19. Watch
4. saw	12. seeing	20. Look
5. looking	13. watch	21. watching
6. looks	14. see	22. Watch
7. watch	15. Look	23. look … see
8. watch	16. watch	24. watching
		25. see

Collocations Make Pictures

word for word
word for **word**

You have my **word**.

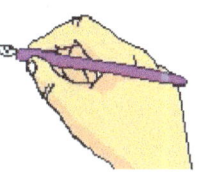

Microsoft **Word**

Give the **word**.

word of mouth

Collocations represent ideas.
   Word for word means copy exactly.
   Give the word means permission.
   You have my word means I promise.
   Microsoft Word is computer software.
   Word of mouth is communication by speaking.

The number of words any single word collocates with is limited. Some words exist only inside rare collocations – moot only exists in moot point, scrimp only exists in scrimp and save.

English is made of tiny groups of words that go together for no reason and make pictures.

Students need to ask:

What is the expression for that?

(He laughed his head off.)

www.thompsonlanguagecenter.com

Abstract Thinking Skills

Now that students know English comes in little word packages that don't make logical sense, they need to develop special skills to bridge the gap between the literal words and the abstract messages in English. They need some abstract thinking skills.

Not to put too fine a point on it, but grammar is a linear process and English communication isn't.

In philosophical terminology, abstraction is the thought process wherein ideas are distanced from objects.

Abstraction uses a strategy of simplification, wherein formerly concrete details are left ambiguous, vague, or undefined; thus effective communication about things in the abstract requires an intuitive or common experience between the communicator and the communication recipient.
Wikipedia

To abstract is to take qualities from a literal or concrete image and apply them in a different context.

To native speakers, it's cold is about the weather, and she's cold can be a judgement.

English is not a linear language. It would help students immensely if that were explained to them. Put away the verb tenses for a minute and teach a few riddles. Some basic word order is essential, but learners need to use their *lateral thinking skills* to communicate proficiently with native English speakers. Because English is abstract, tiny little groups of words or *collocations* transmit ideas quickly and vividly.

The early bird catches the worm.

PAINT THE TOWN RED

In the dog house

*Our language, although structured, has many examples of breaks in logic or subversions of patterns. We can use our cleverness to turn this **weakness** of language into a source of delight.*
Delightful Homonyms

Lateral Thinking Exercise

What's black and white and red all over?
The newspaper (*read* all over)

What is the longest word in the dictionary?
The word s*mile*s because there is a *mile* between each s.

Jokes and Riddles

Riddle: What did the big chimney say to the little chimney?
   A: You are too young to smoke.

1. What do you call a light-colored bucket?

2. Why did the king draw straight lines?

3. What do you call rabbit fur?

4. What kind of hot drink did the golfer order?

5. How did Bambi begin a letter to his mother?

6. Why did the teacher wear sunglasses?

7. Why did Silly Sally stop tap dancing?

8. What has four wheels and flies?

9. What would happen if the eye doctor came into the classroom?

10. Why was the rooster named Robinson?

Answers:
1. pale (pail) 2. Because he was a ruler.
3. hair (hare) 4. tea (tee)
5. dear (deer)
6. Because her students were so bright.
7. She kept falling in the sink.
8. A garbage truck.
9. She would check the pupils.
10. Because he 'crew so.'

English is Idiomatic

Special groups of words have many different names like *phrasal verbs*, *idioms*, *expressions*… but they are all forms of word groups that work together to make images. These word groups are called collocations and they come from a wide variety of origins. It is not necessary to know the origin in order to use a collocation correctly.

Phrasal verbs: look at, put on, put up with…

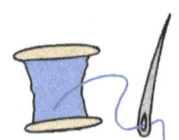

Adages: a stitch in time saves nine, a penny saved is a penny earned…

Expressions: once in a blue moon, time flies…

Lingo: What's up? Talk to the hand, couch potato…

Fables: *The Fox and the Grapes* – sour grapes

Parables: *The Wolf and the Shepherd Boy* – cry wolf

Fairy tales: Once upon a time, *Sleeping Beauty*, happily ever after…

Literature: *Paradise Lost*, *Great Expectations*, To be or not to be…

History: That old chestnut, I have a dream, Four score and seven years…

    Nautical – A red sky at night is a sailor's delight, a loose cannon, three sheets to the wind…

    Agricultural – take the bull by the horns, a wolf in sheep's clothing, you can lead a horse to water…

    Military – Don't shoot till you see the whites of their eyes, war is hell, discretion is the better part of valor…

Religion: loaves and the fishes, turn water into wine, walk on water, parting of the Red Sea…

Movies, songs & pop culture: We'll always have Paris, make my day, not in Kansas any more, frankly my dear…

Business: bull market, office politics, time is money, corporate ladder.

Collocations generate powerful images. **The exact image is different for everyone.**

English as an idiomatic language is much vaguer than second-language learners realize. Native speakers ***infer*** ideas with as few words as possible using collocations from every corner of our culture. Much of the time, native speakers aren't sure of what is being said – that's how politicians get elected. Most of **English is implied** and therefore subject to (or lost in) interpretation. English is subjective. Everyone has their own experiences. People ***filter*** what they hear through their past experiences. No two people experience the same event in exactly the same way.

Collocation Multiple Choice
Advanced

Read the collocation and circle the answer that means the same thing.

1) **When pigs fly**
   a) It's never going to happen.   b) a medical miracle
   c) a stock market recovery

2) **Dinner is on me.**
   a) Food spilled on me.   b) I cooked dinner.   c) I am paying for dinner.

3) **A bad break**
   a) bone fracture   b) short or missed coffee time   c) bad luck

4) **Threw a party**
   a) hosted a party   b) didn't go to a party you said you would
   c) went to a party but didn't stay long

5) **He's a brick**.
   a) He's reliable.   b) He is a stone mason.   c) He is stupid.

6) **Every cloud has a silver lining.**
   a) It's a weather report.   b) Every misfortune has some benefit.
   c) Buy quality silverware.

7) **Shake a leg**
   a) Please pass the chicken.   b) Iron your pants.   c) Hurry up.

8) I'm going to give him **a piece of my mind.**
   a) signed your organ donor card   b) I'm going to yell at him.
   c) I'm going to have a conversation with him.

9) **Take the bull by the horn**
   a) Take action.   b) Catch a farm animal.
   c) Don't listen to nonsense.

10) She looks at the world **through rose-colored glasses.**
    a) Her favorite color is pink.   b) Her name is Rose.   c) She's optimistic.

Multiple Choice Answer Key

1) a   2) c   3) c   4) a   5) a   6) b   7) c   8) b   9) a   10) c

Teacher Page   Expressions

Language is the Tip of the Iceberg

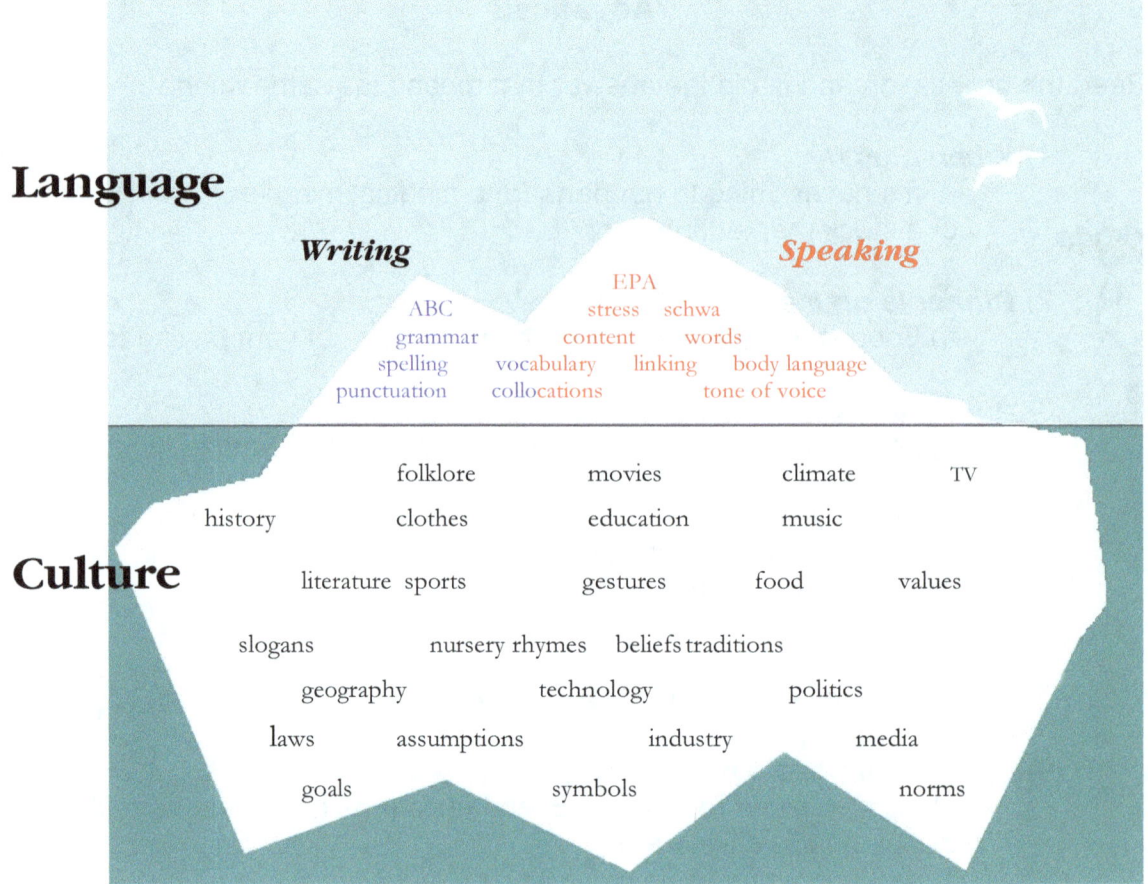

Understanding comes from under the surface.

There is a limit to how far grammar and spelling are going to take anyone learning English. Students have to take responsibility for experiencing Western culture.

Language comes from shared experiences.

Students only learn *about* language in books and school. Fluency comes from outside school, out in the culture of the language being learned. Don't be shy. Start at the beginning with content words and cartoons. Be kind to yourself.

© Judy Thompson 2009

Expressions   Student Page

Get into the Culture –
The Language Will Follow

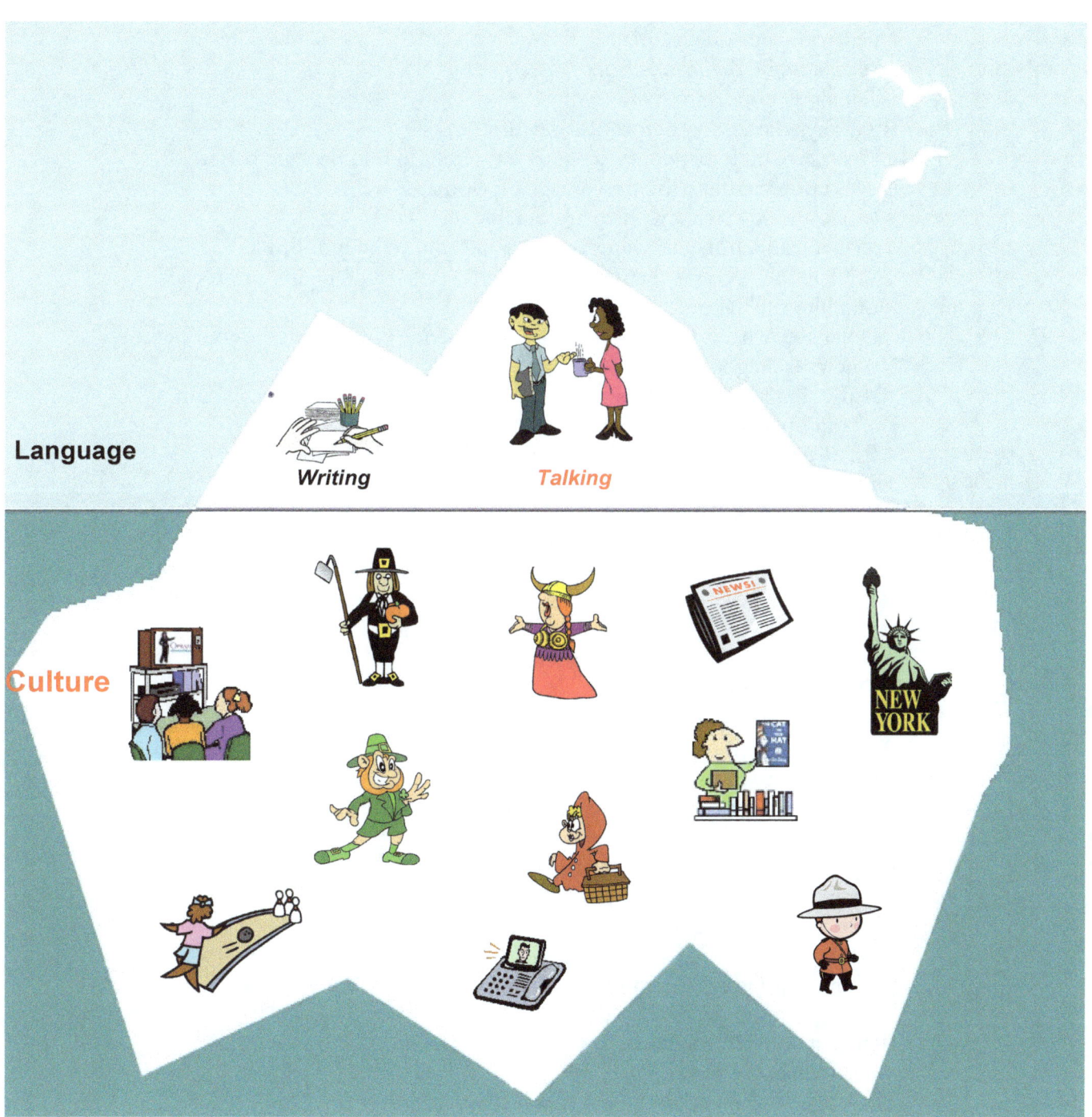

Abstract Thinking is Learned

Here are twenty common expressions and their meanings. Students will have more fun with the exercise on the opposite page if they know the original expression and what it means.

1. Don't change horses .... in the middle of the stream.
   Stay with your original plan.
2. Strike .... while the iron is hot.
   Timing is important.
3. It's always darkest .... before the dawn.
   Don't give up hope; things seem worst – right before they get better.
4. Never underestimate the power of .... a woman.
   Don't misjudge what women are capable of.
5. You can lead a horse to water but .... you can't make him drink.
   With all the necessary arrangements made, a plan still might not proceed.
6. Don't bite the hand .... that feeds you.
   Don't speak badly about your boss or your company; they write your paycheck.
7. No news is .... good news.
   If you don't hear any news to the contrary, things are probably all right.
8. You can't teach an old dog ....new tricks.
   It's difficult for older people to change the way they do things.
9. The pen is mightier than the .... sword.
   Words are more powerful than weapons.
10. An idle mind is .... the devil's playground.
    When you don't have enough work to do, there is time to get into trouble.
11. Where there's smoke .... there's fire.
    The smoke is a sign there is something more serious going on.
12. A penny saved is .... a penny earned.
    Don't waste money.
13. Two's company, three's .... a crowd.
    There is no possibility of intimacy between two people when a third person is around.
14. Don't put off till tomorrow what .... you can do today.
    Do it now.
15. Laugh and the world laughs with you; cry and .... you cry alone.
    People like to be around happy people, not sad ones.
16. There are none so blind as .... those who will not see.
    Denial
17. Children should be seen and not .... heard.
    Noisy children are rude.
18. If at first you don't succeed ... try and try again.
    Persistence is a good thing.
19. You get out of something only what you .... put into it.
    Take action; the more you do, the better the result.
20. Better late than .... never.
    Doing something late is not good, but it's better than not doing it at all.

© Judy Thompson 2009

Fun with Collocations

A first-grade teacher in Virginia presented each child in her class the first half of a well-known proverb and asked them to come up with the remainder of the proverb. Their responses below are **literal**.

Native speakers think this is hysterical!

What is the original expression for each of the following?

1. Don't change horses .... *until they stop running*.
2. Strike while the .... *bug is close*.
3. It's always darkest .... *before Daylight Savings*.
4. Never underestimate the power of .... *termites*.
5. You can lead a horse to water but .... *how?*
6. Don't bite the hand .... *that looks dirty*.
7. No news is .... *impossible*.
8. You can't teach an old dog .... *math*.
9. The pen is mightier than the .... *pigs*.
10. An idle mind is .... *the best way to relax*.
11. Where there's smoke there's .... *pollution*.
12. A penny saved is .... *not much*.
13. Two's company, three's .... *the Musketeers*.
14. Don't put off till tomorrow what .... *you put on to go to bed*.
15. Laugh and the world laughs with you, cry and .... *you have to blow your nose*.
16. There are none so blind as .... *Stevie Wonder*.
17. Children should be seen and not .... *spanked or grounded*.
18. If at first you don't succeed ... *get new batteries*.
19. You get out of something only what you .... *see in the picture on the box*.
20. Better late than .... *pregnant*.

If you didn't do well with the expressions, don't worry about it. It takes a lifetime to *get* English, even if it's your native language. Sometime after the age of six, native speakers develop the **abstract** quality of English.

www.thompsonlanguagecenter.com

Why I Don't Like the Dictionary

The trouble with the dictionary is that you have to know how a word is spelled before you can look it up to see how it is spelled. Will Cuppy

That is not the only problem with the dictionary. You have to know how to **spell** the word in order to look it up, but you also have to know what it **sounds** like, what it **means** and how it's **used**. You can't use a dictionary unless you don't need to.

Native speakers may use a dictionary to **verify** words they already have a sense of, which isn't that helpful because the dictionary uses words they don't understand in the definitions. Then, they have to look those up .... actually, they don't bother because it's too much work. They just ask someone. Most native English speakers pick up a dictionary less than once a year. Non-native speakers have difficulty using a regular dictionary at all.

Learner Dictionaries

There have been two giant steps forward here. **Step 1** is *a **learner dictionary*** that provides **simple** definitions for the most common English words and demonstrates **how** each word is used. For **pronunciation**, the dreaded International Phonetic Alphabet (IPA) is **replaced** with a keyboard system. (and voice recordings online). **Step 2** is a ***sound dictionary***. Words are catalogued by ***main vowel sound*** (Thompson Vowel Chart pg 55). **How Do You Say?** (Amazon) includes thousands of common ***expressions***.

English and Computers

Computers can't translate English because English is abstract and computers are literal. There is a common expression **out of sight, out of mind** for the notion that you don't think of something or someone when they aren't there. Ask for a definition of that expression from a computer and it gives **blind and crazy,** which isn't even close.

Entry from the *New Oxford Advanced Learner Dictionary*

Cat: /kaet/ *noun*
  1 a small animal with soft fur that people often keep as a pet. Cats catch and kill birds and mice: cat food – see also KITTEN, TOMCAT **2** a wild animal of the cat family: the cat. IDM be the cats' whiskers/py'jamas (*informal*) to be the best thing, person, idea, etc.: *He thinks he's the cat's whiskers* = he has a high opinion of himself. Let the cat out of the bag = to tell a secret carelessly or by mistake: *I wanted it to be a surprise but my sister let the cat out of the bag.* Like a cat on hot bricks (BrE) = be very nervous. *She was like a cat on hot bricks before her driving test.* Like a cat that's got the cream (BrE) (US like a cat that got/ate/ swallowed the canary) = very pleased with yourself. SYN SMUG look like sth the cat brought/dragged in *(informal)* = to look dirty and untidy. Not have/stand a cat in hell's chance of doing sth = to have no chance at all. Play a game of cat and mouse with sb / play a cat and mouse game with sb = to play a cruel game with sb in your power by changing your behavior very often, so that they become nervous and do not know what to expect. Put the cat among the pigeons (BrE) = to say or do sth that is likely to cause trouble. When the cat's away the mice will play (saying) = people enjoy themselves more and behave with greater freedom when the person in charge of them is not there – more at CURIOSITY, RAIN, ROOM n, WAY n.

There are two lines about the **literal** meaning of cat and more than thirteen lines about the **abstract** use of cat. Some expressions with cat are missing, like cat got your tongue? but there are references to more idiomatic uses of the word. The learner dictionaries are useful for English students when they use keyboard symbols for pronunciation, and show the words in context, with simple text that can be easily understood.

Real English Exercise

Underline the collocations in the passage by Catherine Dunphy from the *Toronto Star*, July 30, 2007.

Brenda Reble: Dedicated ESL instructor known for her love of community

News | Teacher's dinners brought together good friends, good food

Life threw Brenda Reble a couple of bad breaks – so in turn she threw dinner parties. Wonderful dinner parties in which her adult English as a Second Language students mingled with her friends and fellow teachers, talking about what they dreamed of and what they cared about over her home-cooked feasts. Reble's dinner parties represented everything she lived for – community, caring, cooking. And so friend and fellow ESL teacher Anne Erickson urged everyone at the celebration of Reble's life to throw a dinner party or two in her honour.

A child of missionaries, Reble had once told Erickson she regarded her dinners as her outreach work because it was there she brought together people from all over the world. "Community was her passion," said her father, retired Lutheran minister Eric Reble. "She wanted people to be community and family and to meet. A dinner is so true of what Brenda would love to see happen."

In her 30 years of teaching ESL – until last year she was a fixture at the Jones Ave. Adult Center – Reble cajoled, inspired, coached and mentored her students. Her classes were electric, her students totally engaged.

There was no talking down, no carefully drawn out syllables in her English classes. She was a feminist, strong-willed, opinionated. In her classes they discussed Sharia Law, cloning, what justifies war, gay rights. She taught them about their rights as tenants and how to complain effectively; she was very protective of abused women.

In her spare time and on her own dime, she helped them work up their résumés, coached them through their first job interviews, used her connections to find them work. And always, she cooked for them, bringing baking to classes.

The eldest of four children, Reble was raised in a hill station in south India. Back in Canada at university she was president of the international student association when she suffered a grand mal epileptic seizure; she had to take heavy medication the rest of her life, which contributed to a permanent weight gain. A borderline diabetic, she still couldn't give up the food that was so central to her life's credo.

She was a qualified teacher who could have taught in a high school and earned 30 per cent more than she did as an ESL instructor, but she loved teaching adults.

"If Toronto is known for anything it's that we welcome the world," said her brother Peter. "The ESL teachers are the front line. They are the unsung heroes."

Reprinted with permission - Torstar Syndication Services

Teacher Page Expressions

Real English is *Fraught with* Collocations

All oral and all *written* English are collocations – it's the way English is put together. The headlines in the newspaper tomorrow morning are going to be collocations.

Collocations/expressions and accents are why learned language speakers don't sound like native English speakers. Collocations/expressions are also why foreigners don't understand native English speakers.

Native speakers are often poor at ensuring that they are understood in international discussions. They tend to think they need to avoid longer words, when comprehension problems are more often caused by their use of colloquial and metaphorical English.   Michael Skapinker

Answer Key

BRENDA REBLE: **Dedicated ESL instructor known for her love of community**
News | Teacher's dinners brought together good friends, good food

Life threw Brenda Reble a couple of bad breaks – so in turn she threw dinner parties. Wonderful dinner parties in which her adult English as a Second Language students mingled with her friends and fellow teachers, talking about what they dreamed of and what they cared about over her home-cooked feasts.

Reble's dinner parties represented everything she lived for – community, caring, cooking.

And so friend and fellow ESL teacher Anne Erickson urged everyone at the celebration of Reble's life to throw a dinner party or two in her honour.

A child of missionaries, Reble had once told Erickson she regarded her dinners as her outreach work because it was there she brought together people from all over the world.

"Community was her passion," said her father, retired Lutheran minister Eric Reble. "She wanted people to be community and family and to meet. A dinner is so true of what Brenda would love to see happen."

In her 30 years of teaching ESL – until last year she was a fixture at the Jones Ave. Adult Center – Reble cajoled, inspired, coached and mentored her students. Her classes were electric, her students totally engaged.

There was no talking down, no carefully drawn out syllables in her English classes. She was a feminist, strong-willed, opinionated. In her classes they discussed Sharia Llaw, cloning, what justifies war, gay rights. She taught them about their rights as tenants and how to complain effectively; she was very protective of abused women.

In her spare time and on her own dime, she helped them work up their résumés, coached them through their first job interviews, used her connections to find them work. And always, she cooked for them, bringing baking to classes.

The eldest of four children, Reble was raised in a hill station in south India. Back in Canada at university she was president of the international student association when she suffered a grand mal epileptic seizure; she had to take heavy medication the rest of her life, which contributed to a permanent weight gain. A borderline diabetic, she still couldn't give up the food that was so central to her life's credo.

She was a qualified teacher who could have taught in a high school and earned 30 per cent more than she did as an ESL instructor, but she loved teaching adults.

"If Toronto is known for anything it's that we welcome the world," said her brother Peter. "The ESL teachers are the front line. They are the unsung heroes."

© Judy Thompson 2009

Volunteering

***Even more than language is the access to culture,
culture is the access to language.***

To learn a language, participate in the culture – get a hobby, watch movies and volunteer.

If you cook – you can prepare meals for the homeless.

If you have office skills – you can keep books for a charity.

If you like children – the local school can use your help.

If you have carpentry skills,
 build a set for local little theatre…

Working for no money is **volunteering**. This isn't a joke; volunteering is part of western culture. Volunteering in a field that interests you can give you the language you need for future employment. Volunteer experience counts as *work experience* on your resumé, and you can get a letter of reference from your supervisor (if you did a good job, got along well with others, always arrived on time…) Many people are hired by companies where they volunteered.

Volunteers also feel useful and happy. It's a great way to make friends. Volunteering helps us all appreciate what we **do** have and what we **can** do, and our world gets bigger.

Students will learn more about *speaking* English when they volunteer than they ever will in school.

The volunteering experience serves as a classroom for real English and can be a stepping stone to a new career.

Teacher Page   Expressions

Home Study

The greatest sign of success for a teacher is to be able to say,
The children are now working as if I did not exist.
                                        Maria Montessori

HOT TIP
Encourage students to watch the same movie over and over, like children do. Children know what is going to happen after the first time they watch a movie, but they watch the same one over and over again for the language. Have your students do the same.

The top three most frequently quoted movies of all time are:
> *Casablanca* (1943) with Humphry Bogart and Lauren Bacall
> *The Wizard of Oz* (1939) with Judy Garland
> *Gone With the Wind* (1939) with Vivian Leigh and Clark Gable

Lists of popular movies are available on sites like the American Film Institute.

The first time students watch, they may understand about 20%; the second time, 30%; the fourth or fifth time, 80%. They may never get more than 80%, but 80% is great.

Humor is the test.
When you *get jokes* or *make jokes* in English, you have the language.

Western Culture in their Homes

Learners can play 15 minutes of a video, rewind, play it again, and rewind it again. Call it *studying*. **Groundhog Day** (1993) with Bill Murray and Andie MacDowell plays the same day over and over again. Students should have movies playing in their homes all the time.

Highly Recommended Movies Based on True Stories:

The Miracle Worker (1962) – a black and white movie about the life of Helen Keller, starring Patty Duke and Anne Bancroft. Helen Keller was a blind and deaf girl who needed language, and once she got it, she changed the world.

Door to Door (2002) – Bill Porter (played by William H. Macy) was a *door-to-door* salesman with cerebral palsy. Language was one of the many obsticales Bill overcame.

Erin Brockovich (2000) starring Julia Roberts about a single mom who became a legal secretary, found her voice and brought down a California power company

Hollywood tends to exaggerate true stories but here are some *true* stories I like anyways:

> *Rainman* (1988)   *Beautiful Mind* (2001)
> *Patch Adams* (1998)   *October Sky* (1999)
> *Apollo 13* (1995)   *Pursuit of Happyness* (2006)
> *Catch Me if You Can* (2002)   *A League of Their Own* (1992)
> *Aviator* (2004)   *The Sound of Music* (1965)
> *Seabiscuit* (2003)   *World's Fastest Indian* (2005)
> *Schindler's List* (1993)   *The Rookie* (2002)
> *Walk the Line* (2005)   *Chariots of Fire* (1981)
> *The Blind Side* (2009)   *Braveheart* (1995)

© Judy Thompson 2009

Go Ahead, Talk to Your Neighbor

No one cares about your accent (remember Chapter Two.) Content words are enough (Chapter Three.) Since grammar is not important for *speaking*, don't worry about that either (Chapter Five.) So go ahead and talk to your neighbors.

Don't be afraid. They are going to understand you, and no one is going to ask anything *personal*.

When you go to a coffee shop, they are going to ask you what you want in your coffee. If it's not busy, they may make a comment about the weather.

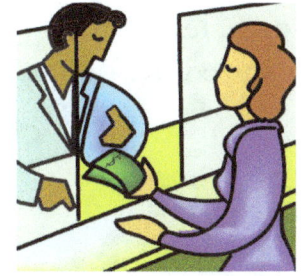

Say **Hi** to the teller at the bank. They are going to ask you what you want them to do with your money. They are not going to ask you how much you weigh.

Talk to your neighbor over the fence.
He is not going to ask how big your feet are.
He is just going to smile and talk about the weather.
It's western culture.

The grocer is going to ask you if you want another bag.
He is not going to ask why you wear funny clothes.

Your co-workers at the water cooler are only talking about what they saw last night on TV. Join in. Don't worry.
They are not going to ask you how much you paid for your house.

One must learn by doing the thing.
For though you think you know it, you have no certainty until you try.
Sophocles

What Students Need to Know about Collocations

- Study words in groups, not individually. It's very important.

- Fluency requires thousands of collocations or groups of words.

- There is no substitute for learning through practice outside the classroom.

- *How do you say?* Is a dictionary of **expressions** created for ESL learners by ESL teachers. Entries are organized by sound not spelling. (Amazon)

*Making mental connections is our most crucial learning tool, the essence of human intelligence; to forge links; to go beyond the given; to see patterns, relationships, **context**.*
— Marilyn Ferguson

Context and fixed word groups (expressions) are how English is put together and how it must be studied for mastery (fluency).

In
an apple for the teacher,
the apple means
acknowledgement.

It represents everything good and positive about education.

In the
Garden of Eden,
the apple means
temptation.

Expressions

Laundry List

English is idiomatic.

What that means for the student is:

Learn words in groups.

Chapter Five
Collocations

1. The meaning of individual words doesn't count for much in English.
2. **Context** is the situation, conversation or text around any given word.
3. Context gives individual words their meaning.
4. English comes in small, fixed groups of words called **collocations.**
5. The most impactful subcategory of collocation is **expressions**.
6. Expressions don't always seem logical; they are cultural and idiomatic.
7. English fluency is a combination of context and expressions.
8. Language is rooted in culture. To become proficient in a language, you must participate in it authentically.
9. A good way to experience a culture is to volunteer in it in a field that interests you.

Five Rules for Speaking English

There, that's it. There are **five rules for** *speaking* **English.**

1. Letters don't represent sounds. The English Phonetic Alphabet represents sounds and is a useful tool for learners.

2. English is a stress-based language. Intelligibility is a function of word stress.

3. Content words are important and must be stressed.

4. Native English speakers run words together predictably, in a process called linking (aka connected speech).

5. English comes in small, fixed groups of words called collocations. The most notable category of these fixed word groups is expressions.

These five rules explain only about 20% of how native English speakers converse.

Chapter Six looks at the missing piece that makes up approximately 80% of English communication.

Chapter Six
Body Language
Non-Verbal Communication

There was speech in their dumbness, language in their very gesture.
William Shakespeare

CHAPTER SIX

Body Language
or
Non-Verbal Communication

There are over a million words used in English, far more than in any other language. The ridiculously huge lexicon, the weak relationship between letters and sounds, and the abstract nature of English leaves this language vague and difficult to master. **English is crazy.** Perhaps by default, non-verbal cues have become a vital part of the language. English speakers rely heavily on specialized *voice qualities, facial expressions* (including *eye contact, gestures, personal space* and *body movements*) to get their messages across. *Body language* works closely with *spoken* English to produce fluent conversation.

Body Language
Chapter 6
80%

Chapters 1 to 5
20%

The varied use of **high, middle** and **low notes** ♪ identify *important words* and serve the same function as *punctuation*.

Volume and *tone of voice* convey *emotion.*

Body movements and *gestures* are more *powerful* communication tools *than all the other components, including words, combined*.

Telephone conversations and radio programs are all but impossible for ESL beginners to understand – because they *can't see the speaker*.

Communicating in English involves a lot of *guessing.*

Body language provides a lot of clues.

The British television character, *Mr. Bean* (played by Rowan Atkinson) is an ideal example of how powerfully and perfectly people can express themselves without any words at all.

Voice Sounds and Body Language

When is he finished talking?

When he **lowers his voice**, they will know he is finished.

(They look as if they have been waiting a long time.)

How is she feeling?

We can also *guess* how people feel from how they use their **voice**.

What can we *guess* about this woman, even when we can't hear her?

Is she happy?

We don't know what she is saying on the telephone, and the person she is talking to can't see her, but everyone knows she is upset from the volume and **tone of her voice**.

What do these faces say?

We can *figure out* whether these people are glad, sad or mad from what we **see**.

Rule #6   Communication does not need words.

Context. body language, tone of voice, and facial expressions are some of the strongest cues native speakers provide in the *guessing game* of English conversation.

♪ Notes ♪

Native speakers use **three regular musical notes** constantly in **normal** *speaking*
Two of them were mentioned in Chapter Two on *stress*.

A **high note** tells the listener this is an **important word**.
All **content words** have a **high note**.

A **middle note** indicates **unimportant words** and syllables, and native speakers have learned to disregard information at this pitch.

/buh NA nuh/   The vowel sounds of **middle notes** is *schwa* /uh/.

There is also a very important **low note**.

The **low note** indicates they've **finished** *speaking*.
The **end** of every **statement** and *wh* **question** in English is a very **low note**.
The low note is the equivalent to a period in *writing*.
It never occurs in the middle of a sentence.

Asking Questions

Wh questions end on the same low note as statements.

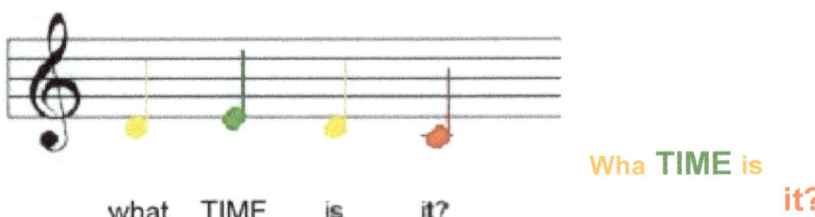

Body Language — Student Page

♪ Notes ♪

Spoken English uses three main notes.

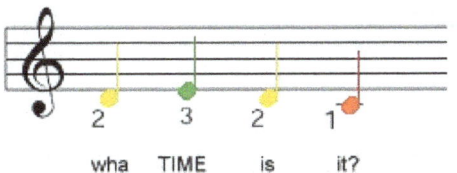

Statements and **wh** or information questions always end on low red notes.

What do you want to do?	Wha da ya **WAN**na **DO**?
I have to go to the store.	I **HAVE** ta **GO** ta tha **STORE**.
I want to get some milk.	I **WAN**na **GET** sa **MILK**.
She is as free as a bird.	She zaz **FREE** as a **BIRD**.
What do you take in your tea?	Wha da ya **TAKE** in your **TEA**?

Telling Your Story

Lowering your voice to a really low note tells the person you are talking to that you are **finished speaking**. Then it's their turn to respond in the conversation. You *have the floor* until you drop your voice.

Honey, it wasn't my fault ... There was this big curve ...
I wasn't going too fast ... but a cat ran in front of the car...
I tried to stop ... but my foot slipped off the brake ...
I steered around it ... but it was scared ...
It kinda crouched on the road ... I didn't want to hit it ...
I swerved ... just a bit ... My tires barely touched
the shoulder ... and there was this post.
         I'm sorry.

www.thompsonlanguagecenter.com

Yes/No Questions

An *extra* **high note** at the end of statement or question means:

The answer is **yes** or **no**.

Do you want to come with me?   Da ya WANna COME with ME?
Are these on sale?   Are these on sale?
Would you like fries with that?   Would you like fries with that?

Any word or sentence can be expressed as a *yes/no question* by *rising intonation.*

COFFEE?

Special Note for Spanish Speakers

Spanish is a beautiful logical language that basically uses two notes (yellow and green), and the music of the language goes up and down like waves on a choppy sea. *When statements end on the higher of the two notes.* **In English, this means** *Answer me – yes or no.* If you ask a Spanish speaker an information question and they answer on a high note, they sound unsure.

  Where are ya FROM?   CoLUMbiA ? – sounds like they don't know.

Spanish speakers need to find that low note Co LUM bi a or they sound unsure.

It is very difficult to change programming from a first language. (This is why accents are predictable). To help Spanish-speaking students find and learn the missing low note, here is a little song they will love to learn and the class can sing it as a round for fun. "Row, row, row…" the first three notes of the song are the infamous **low note** missing from the Spanish speaker's first language.

© Judy Thompson 2009

Apple Tree Match Game

Join the dots to the sentences with matching note patterns. There is only one pair of sentences for each note pattern.

The five note patterns are:

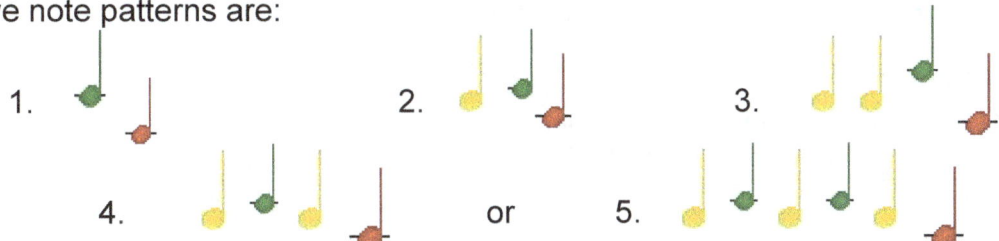

Hint: Each apple will be separated from the others by the connecting lines.

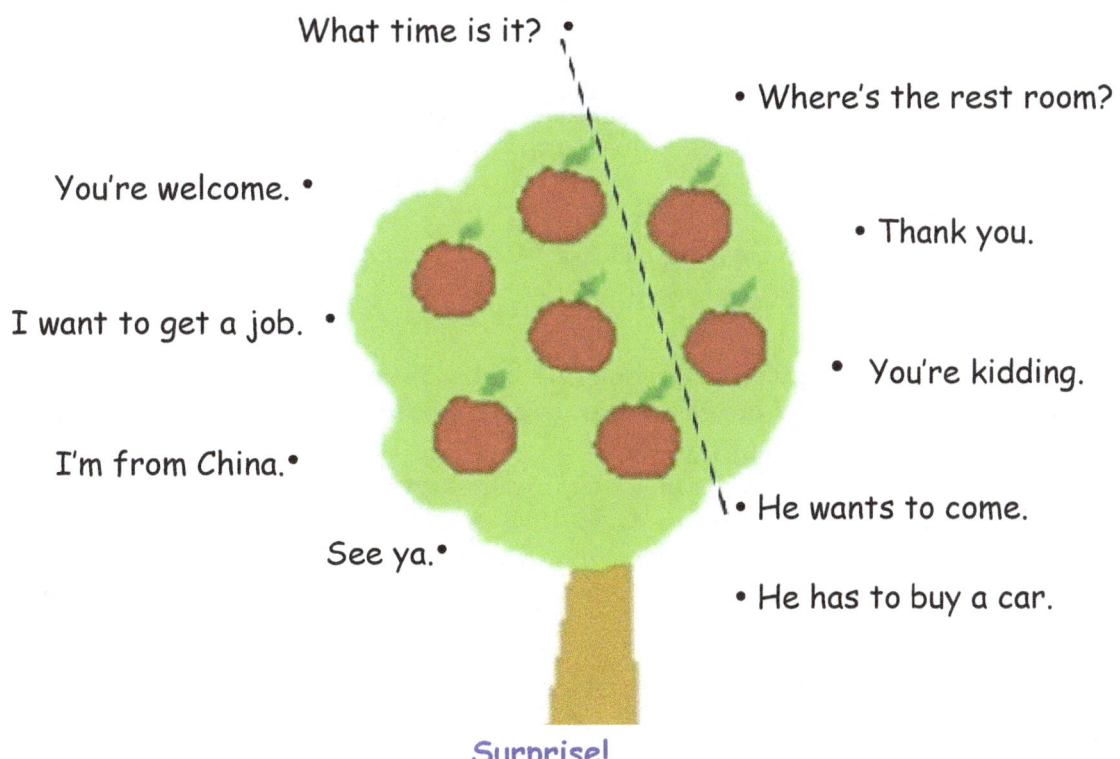

Surprise!

There are two more ♪ notes ♪ used in English, but they are rare. An exclamation mark indicates extreme emotion in *written* English, and the *spoken* counterpart is squealing. Teenage girls and lottery winners make an extremely high-pitched squeaky, OH MY GOD! in their excitement. They called my numbers!

Conversely, an extra low note signifies devastation.
I lost the ticket.

Normal speaking uses three notes, **but two extra notes are around for extreme emotion!**

Tone of Voice

Another *voice quality* native speakers use to communicate is **tone of voice**. Tone of voice is a very powerful tool for communicating *true feelings.* More than words, a person's **tone of voice** tells if they are feeling happy, sad or angry.

In the **How Do You Feel** exercise on the opposite page, notice how men and women or people from diverse cultures have different emotions about the same word or event. When some women squeal **baby** or **wedding**, they can shatter glass. Some men feel that way about sports cars…

Tone of Voice is more Powerful than Words

I'm home!
Think about the husband who comes home late, kisses his wife on the cheek and asks her how her day was.
She folds her arms, shrugs her shoulders, stares at the ground and mumbles,
Fine.
How do you think her day was?

If he is not a complete idiot, he'll ask, What's wrong?
and she'll snap at him, Nothing.

He knows there is something very wrong. If he has been married for a long time, he will ***ignore her words and listen to her tone of voice.*** He may pursue the matter with more questions… and perhaps flowers. ☺
- When the words and the tone don't match – ***trust the tone.***
- Listen to what people **mean** as opposed to what they **say**.

The most important thing in communication is hearing what isn't being said.
Anonymous

Social Convention – Matching Tone

It's a cultural convention. Westerners reply to someone in the same tone of voice they were greeted in. If a cheerful waitress squeaks, Hi! in a chirpy, happy voice, everyone responds in a chipper Howdy doo!

A grumpy server groans, Hu llo like it's his last day on earth, and everyone grumbles right back.

Newcomers who find North Americans unfriendly should try using a higher tone of voice!

Answer Key

What TIME is it • He WANTS to come   You're KIDding • You're WELcome
Where's the RESTroom • I'm from CHIna   THANK you • SEE ya
He HAS to BUY a car • I WANT to GET a job

Tone of Voice Expresses Emotion

High tones express **positive** messages, and **low tones** convey **negative** ones. How the speaker **feels** about a subject is communicated by the level of voice when talking about it, which can be put on a scale from +5 to -5.

How was the party?

+ 5	**Fantastic!**
4	Great
3	Good
2	**Fine**
1	Okay
0	So-so
- 1	All right
- 2	**Not so good**
- 3	Bad
- 4	Terrible
- 5	The host died.

Words like **fantastic**, **wonderful**, and **party** are **happy words** and are naturally expressed with a high tone of voice all the time.

Negative things like **death, war** and **cancer** are expressed with a very low tone of voice – the lower the tone, the stronger the negative expression of emotion.

Words that are neutral or with no emotional charge are uttered in a neutral tone of voice – **so-so, table** and **floor**.

How Do You Feel?

Rate the following words from +5 to -5 according to your feelings about them. Then say the words to a partner and have them *guess* how you feel.

wonderful	party	sore throat
wedding	snow	baby
music	friends	accident
desk	fantastic	funeral
mother	cooking	fat
table	cousin	dog
fun	school	police
Obama	taxes	problem
pencil	soccer	needle
test	lottery	money
husband/wife	shopping	shoes
chocolate	winter	holiday
divorce	court	laundry
cricket	Porsche	mother-in-law (This is my favorite.)

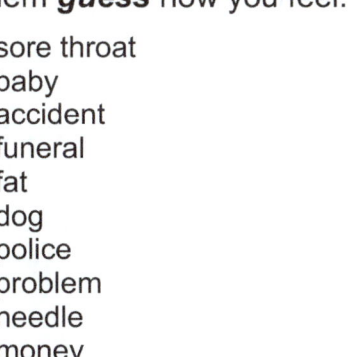
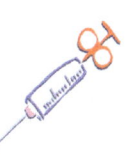

Notice the answers that are the same for men/women, older/younger, or different cultures; but also notice the answers that are different.☺

www.thompsonlanguagecenter.com

Body Language

Besides their voices, native speakers use facial expressions and eye contact as important tools to communicate what they are thinking and feeling.

The expression a woman wears on her face is far more important than the clothes she wears on her back.
                                                                  Dale Carnegie

Although facial expressions for the six major emotions – anger, fear, disgust, sadness, happiness and surprise – are universal, other non-verbal behaviors vary across cultures.

Body language is central to understanding English. Native speakers are unaware of the amount on information they convey using their faces and bodies. It is almost impossible for ESL learners to understand radio programs or telephone conversations, simply because they **can't see** the speaker.

The Eyes Have It

People express themselves with their faces.

Emoticons have come a long way since the original smiley face. The exercise on the opposite page gives a small indication of the versatility of changing tiny lines on a cartoon face to represent a vast array of human emotions.

The very earliest known examples of this graphic are attributed to Harvey Ball, who devised the face in 1963 for the insurance firm, State Mutual Life Assurance. Ball never attempted to use, promote or trademark the image; it fell into the public domain in the United States before this could be accomplished. As a result, Ball never made any profit for the iconic image beyond his initial $45 fee.

Internet Facial Expressions

The Internet has spawned a new breed of communication where letters and symbols are mixed for the fastest, most complete transmission of a message. Creative individuals have combined symbols from a regular keyboard to suggest facial expressions that reflect how they feel.

Here are a few examples:

:) happy   ._. shy |-O bored   =O surprised   :-S confused

Body Language Student Page

How is He?

Circle the word under each face that best describes how the little guy is feeling.

1) happy / suspicious

2) angry / afraid

3) disappointed / bored

4) confused / mean

5) sad / surprised

6) disgusted / exhausted

7) angry / afraid

8) confused / mean

9) sad / surprised

10) disgusted / exhausted

11) disappointed / bored

12) happy / suspicious

www.thompsonlanguagecenter.com

Teacher Page   Body Language

Gestures

I speak two languages, Body and English.
                    Mae West

Mae West was conscious of the *language* she spoke with her body, but most people are not. There are 2,000 common gestures in use in western culture that most native speakers use unconsiously.

Conversation is the slowest form of human communication.
                    Author unknown

Content Words and Gestures

It's natural for people to move their bodies when they speak. Body language punctuates conversation adding meaning and feeling. Native English speakers move specifically on **content words** substantiating the importance of those words. They never move their bodies on function words.

There is a zone in front of the belly button where Western speakers normally gesture with their hands. They never move their hands in front of their eyes or impede eye contact with the person they are speaking with. They may also lean forward or raise their eyebrows… Watch for this the next time English speakers are talking. People consistently move their bodies in conjunction with the message they are trying to convey.

Answer Key

1) happy	2) angry	3) bored	4) mean	5) surprised	6) disgusted
7) afraid	8) confused	9) sad	10) exhausted	11) disappointed	12) suspicious

Body Language — Student Page

People Talk with Their Hands

Look how people use their hands when they communicate!

> ### His Daughter is a Cow
>
> Gestures vary from culture to culture, and students have to *pay attention* to the customs and behaviors of the society where they live. For example, South Americans measure the height of their livestock with a flat hand and the height of person with their hand turned perpendicular to the ground. For a Columbian to see a North American indicating *my daughter is this tall* with a flat hand – it seems like the American is calling his daughter a cow.

Some 2½-Second Rules in Western Culture

Handshakes are very important in Western culture.
Take a good firm grip. Look the other person in the eye.
2½ pumps up and down. That's it – no variations are acceptable.
Practice the skill of shaking hands with students. It's really important.

Eye Contact: Western people look each other in the eye when they talk – but only at **2½** second intervals.
Staring makes westerners uncomfortable. So does looking away.
The **2½** second rule is a good one to master.

Silence: Westerners have a cultural *intolerance for silence*.
They will wait **2½** seconds for a question to be answered.
Then they will fill the empty space with some noise because they are uncomfortable.
They will either repeat the question, change the subject, or leave.

Umm: The signal western-born people give to indicate they have heard the question and are thinking of an answer is **umm.** Native speakers say **umm** all the time. They are holding their place in the conversation.

Lesson Idea: Teach Students to Say **Umm**

Teacher: **What time is it?**
Student: **Umm**   because it takes longer than 2½ seconds to pull out their phone and check.

Teacher: **What is the capital of Bolivia? India? Nepal?**
The response is always the same – **Ummm** – then the answer.

Umm means *I heard you, I understand the question, and I am thinking of the answer.*

Err is another frequently used grunt packed full of meaning. Delivering unfavorable news is often preceded by **Err** or **Uhh** followed by an explanation.

Boss: **Did you get the report done?**
Me: **Err...** is all the boss needs to hear to know the report isn't done.

What are these Gestures Saying?[8]

Call me.

Hold hand to ear with thumb and little finger sticking out.

1.
Wave hand up and down quickly in front of open mouth.

2.
Point index finger at temple and move in a circular motion.

3.
Hold one hand flat out with the other hand straight up making a T.

4.
Stick thumb straight up and fold fingers in.

5.
Rub stomach in a circular motion while smiling and saying Mmmmmm.

6.
Hand out-stretched, palm flat pointing down toggling from side to side.

7.
Put index finger in and out of open mouth.

8.
Rub thumb back and forth over the second joint of the index finger.

9.
Pass hand quickly above top of head from front to back.

10.
Make zipper motion across tightly closed lips.

[8] This page was illustrated by Heather Ford.

Teacher Page   Body Language

Lesson Idea: Classroom Game of Common Gestures
Charades

Copy these phrases onto separate strips of paper. Fold the strips and put them in a hat. Have the students pick a phase from the hat and *perform* it for the class using only their bodies. NO WORDS! See how long it takes the class to guess the message. Make suggestions as required – perhaps the students can rehearse in the hall with their teacher, one at a time. ☺

No	Hi	Headache
Yes	Goodbye	Bravo!
Stop	Okay	Please
Go away	Good job	What time is it?
How much $ is this?	Hot - Sexy	Spicy food
He's crazy	Good luck	I don't know
Be quiet	I love you.	Slow down
Come here	Stomach ache	This smells terrible
Hurry up	Time out	Shut up
That's bad	Call me	Get out
Pay attention!	Move over	I can't hear you

The Time Has Come

It's time to push the chicks out of the nest. Teachers can fill their students' heads with information, but information is not transformation. At the end of the day, students are responsible for their own education, and the possibility of fluency in English lives outside the classroom. We can only teach them *about* English; they have to *speak* English on their own.

You cannot teach a man anything;
you can only help him find it within himself.
                                    Galileo Galilei

Answer Key

1) Too hot – spicy
2) Someone is crazy
3) Time out – take a break
4) Thumbs up – good
5) Tastes good
6) So-so – neutral feeling
7) Gag me with a spoon – disgusting
8) Money – How much?
9) Over my head – I don't understand
10) My lips are sealed, secret

© Judy Thompson 2009

Home Study
Highly Recommended

Watch romantic, adventure and comedy movies for vocabulary, expressions, body language and Western culture.

Titanic (1997)
Six Days Seven Nights (1998)
The Devil Wears Prada (2006)
Forrest Gump (1994)
The Princess Bride (1987)
Robin Hood Prince of Thieves (1991)
Bend it Like Beckham (2002)
Mrs. Doubtfire (1993)
How to Lose a Guy in 10 Days (2003)
The Gods Must Be Crazy (1980)
The Sixth Sense (1999)
Steel Magnolias (1989)
The Joy Luck Club (1993)
The King's Speech (2010)
The Sound of Music (1965)

Groundhog Day (1993)
The Shawshank Redemption (1995)
Liar Liar (1997)
Witness (1985)
Cast Away (2000)
Meet the Parents (2000)
The Truman Show (1998)
When Harry Met Sally (1989)
Legally Blonde (2001)
My Big Fat Greek Wedding (2002)
Sleepless in Seattle (1993)
My Cousin Vinny (1991)
Pretty Woman (1990)
Nine toFive (1980)
Home Alone (1990)

Anything with Jackie Chan, James Bond, Mr. Bean or Indiana Jones

Animated films are useful for adults learning English too.

Beauty and the Beast (1991)
Aladdin (1992)
Lion King (1994)
Finding Nemo (2003)
Avatar (2009)

Up (2009)
Mulan (1998)
Shrek (2001)
Toy Story (1995)
Snow White (1937)

Become a *Soap* Addict

Daily television **soap operas** are a great way to learn English.

- The characters stay the same.
- The plot moves slowly.
- The drama is exaggerated and easy to follow.
- There are several simultaneous story lines running at once for variety.

The story lines are printed daily on www.soapcentral.com to follow along or to help you catch up if you miss an episode.

Remember: **REPEAT what the actors are saying, especially if you don't understand them. It increases understanding and decreases accent.**

Teacher Page   Body Language

Strategies

The Jerk Lesson

Be realistic with students and prepare them for the real world that is waiting for them. Sometimes, things go wrong. Sometime, somewhere, someone isn't going to understand them – and sometimes people can be nasty. Talk about this with students. There are special names for people who are mean – they are called *jerks* (or worse). There are two important things for students to remember when they meet nasty people.

1) It isn't personal. Jerks are nasty to everyone. It has nothing to do with students personally or the way they speak English. When you meet a jerk, be grateful you aren't married to them.

2) Statistically, it's great to meet a nasty person. Think about it. What percentage of people in the world are nice? 80%? 90%? When students meet a bus driver or shop clerk who is not nice (and it will happen), they can say:

> Hurray! I met an jerk this morning,
> so the next seven or eight strangers I meet
> are going to be nice!

Basic Communication Breakdown

What to do when Communication isn't Working

- Pardon? – Students can say Pardon or What? Native speakers do this all the time. It's okay to ask someone to repeat what they said.

- Good manners are Excuse me and Please. Native speakers can't resist a polite request: Excuse me, could you please repeat that? or Excuse me, I didn't understand. There is a reason they are called ***magic words!***

- Charades – act it out. Practice hand gestures and *speaking* with animation at home in front of a mirror, then it won't seem so weird in public.

- Write it down or draw a picture.

- Ask for help. Excuse me, could you please help me?

- Most important – Smile!

© Judy Thompson 2009

Body Language   Student Page

Warning!

Some people are nasty.

Someone in this picture is not nice.

I can't tell you which one. It's important to remember that it doesn't have anything to do with you or the way you *speak* English. Jerks are nasty to everyone.

The Worst Problem

Someone Doesn't Understand You

Don't worry. It happens with everyone – native speakers, married couples… Sometimes people don't understand each other. It is a problem with English, not ESL.

   There are a few suggestions
about what to do on the Teacher Page.

Remember:

The problem is not your accent or grammar!

www.thompsonlanguagecenter.com

What Students Need to Know about Body Language

Smile! Smile! Smile!

There are hundreds of languages in the world, but a smile speaks them all.
                                        Anonymous

Other Tips

- Don't nod Yes when you mean No

If someone asks, Do you understand? Don't *nod* or say Yes if the answer is No. To make sure you know what they said, do what native speakers do – **repeat what you heard**. The technique is called *mirroring*. The speaker will tell you if you heard the message that was intended. Getting at the truth saves on confusion and embarrassment down the road.

- If you are not sure, say I don't know

    or   I donno.

- Practice **guessing /asking** people questions about what they mean.

Laundry List

Native speakers communicate with body language.

What that means for the student is:

Watch and learn.

Be aware of social clues.

Chapter Six
Non-Verbal Communication

1. More than **80%** of the message using *spoken* English is non-verbal.

2. Non-verbal communication combines **voice qualities** and **body movements**.

3. Voice qualities indicate **when** a person is **finished** *speaking* and **how** they are **feeling**.

4. *High notes* identify important words; *low notes* are punctuation.

5. *Tone of voice* tells how a person is feeling.

6. *Body language* is more powerful than words.

7. *Body language* varies from culture to culture. Be careful!

8. When in doubt – **smile**!

CONCLUSION

Written English and *Spoken* English are Fundamentally Different

Written English is letters, spelling, grammar, **expressions**, punctuation and formatting.

Spoken English is context, stressed syllables, important words, collocations, **expressions**, voice qualities, body language and guessing.

The only places where the two aspects of the language intersect are **context** and **expressions**.

English is a Secret Language
Breaking the Code

	Writing	*Speaking*	Chapter
Letters	Latin Alphabet a, b, c, d…	English Phonetic Alphabet /ay/, /bey/, /sey/, /dey/…	1
	Each letter is **equally important**.	Unimportant letters are grunted.	2
Words	The meaning of words is in their **spelling** and **context**.	The meaning of words is in their **stressed syllables.**	2
Sentences	**Every word** is **equally important**.	**Important words** are **stressed.**	3
	Spaces separate word units.	Words lose their boundaries from **reduction** and **linking**, pausing interrupts the flow.	4
	Grammar gives structure to **complete thoughts**.	**Content words** suggest **images.**	5
	Adjectives describe **feelings**.	**Tone of voice** indicates **feelings.**	6
	End with a **period**.	End with a **low note.**	6
Punctuation	Period	Low note	6
	Comma – word group	**Pause** – content word group	3
	Question mark • *Wh* – Information question • Yes/No question	 Minor stress – **low note** Extra **high note**	6
	Exclamation Mark	**Very high** or **very low** note	6

© Judy Thompson 2009

Six Elements Define *Spoken* English

There are **six** elements that define *spoken* English as different from **written** English.

1. **Letters**   Ay bEy sEy
   English Phonetic Alphabet

2. **Words**   ba NA na
   Stressed Syllables

3. **Sentences**   a CUP a COFFEE
   Content Words

4. **Linking**   Ca nI ha va bi da vegg?
   Words don't start with vowels

5. **Collocations**   When pigs fly!
   Expressions

6. **Non-verbal communication**   Smile!
   Body Language

English is Crazy is the Context for Speaking English

English is Crazy provides a framework for understanding how native speakers communicate with each other. It defines *spoken* English as different from *written* English. These two parts of the language developed separately and no alphabet unites them, which is unusual. No one ever learned to speak English by reading it (or by reading about it). ☺

To actually speak English, students have to do it on their own.

There is no other way. They have to learn to speak English by *speaking* it and accept that they are going to make some innocent mistakes.

Education is not something which the teacher does…
Maria Montessori

A Student's Guide to Learning English

1. **Memorize** a *basic* vocabulary to help make better guesses about what people might be saying.
2. **Watch TV** and repeat what is heard, even if you don't understand the words.
3. **Watch videos**, rewind and watch them again.
4. **Get a hobby** – have some fun and make some friends with similar interests.
5. **Volunteer** and get free *listening-to-English* lessons. The grammar foundation will build itself unconsciously, as in a first language.
6. **Take it easy** – the expression is, Don't try to run before you can walk.
7. **Accept** that mistakes will happen, but they won't be the end of the world.
8. **Be kind to yourself**. You don't expect anyone to learn anything as fast as you expect yourself to learn English.

It is all going to work out fine.

Conclusion

Books Don't Teach New Skills

No one learned to **play the trombone** by reading a book.

They had to play it.

No one learned to **dance** by reading a book.

They had to move to the music.

No one learned to **ride a bike** by reading a book.

They had to ride it.

No one learned to speak English by reading a book.

They had to speak it.

www.thompsonlanguagecenter.com

POSTSCRIPT
Tomorrow's English

Remember the English-speakers pie chart?

Non-native speakers (pink) outnumber native speakers (blue) by a margin of 4 to 1. The impact of so many learners on the language has rendered Modern English obsolete. Like Old English and Middle English before it, Modern English has had her day and has successfully spawned a new era in the evolution of the English language. In the world market, **International English** is the *lingua franca*[1] of 1.5 billion non-native speakers worldwide.

Internationally, the shocking truth is that English as a first language has become an impediment to communication.

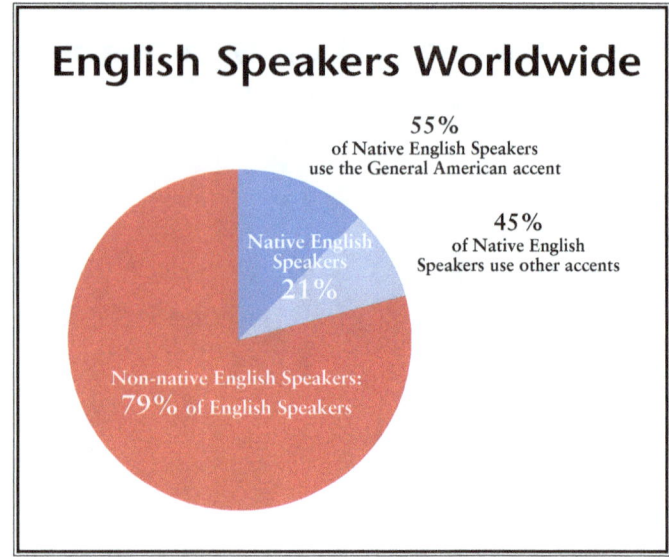

The majority of encounters in English today take place between non-native speakers. Indeed, many business meetings held in English appear to run more smoothly when there are no native English speakers present.

David Graddol, author of English Next

How are non-native speakers (pink part of the pie chart) communicating successfully in English (they understand each other perfectly), but not with native English speakers?

The rules for International English are simple:
- short word list
- simple grammar rules
- body language
- intention

International English uses plain language wihout *expressions* and *linking*.

The biggest shift from Modern English to Global English is in intention. Modern English is about being right; Global English is about being understood. The cornerstone of Global English is *successful communication*, and a statement like **Him and me went to the store** is clear and acceptable. The Victorian obsession with perfect English is gone.

---

[1] A third language systematically used to communicate between persons not sharing a mother tongue.

Postscript

In terms of **English is Crazy**, International English relies on the basic elements of speaking – the sounds of letters, word stress in important words, context and gestures. There are no abstract elements in basic communication. words breaks are pronounced as they are printed with no linking and few expressions.

International English is literal, and native English is abstract.

In the global community, Modern English is simply the old root of a new language where no one has to be perfect to be understood. International communication is a collaborative effort between the listener and the speaker, regardless of race, ethnic background or nationality, and the simple desire to communicate transcends every language barrier.

The End
/ThE yend/

Appendix 1

A Brief History of the English Language

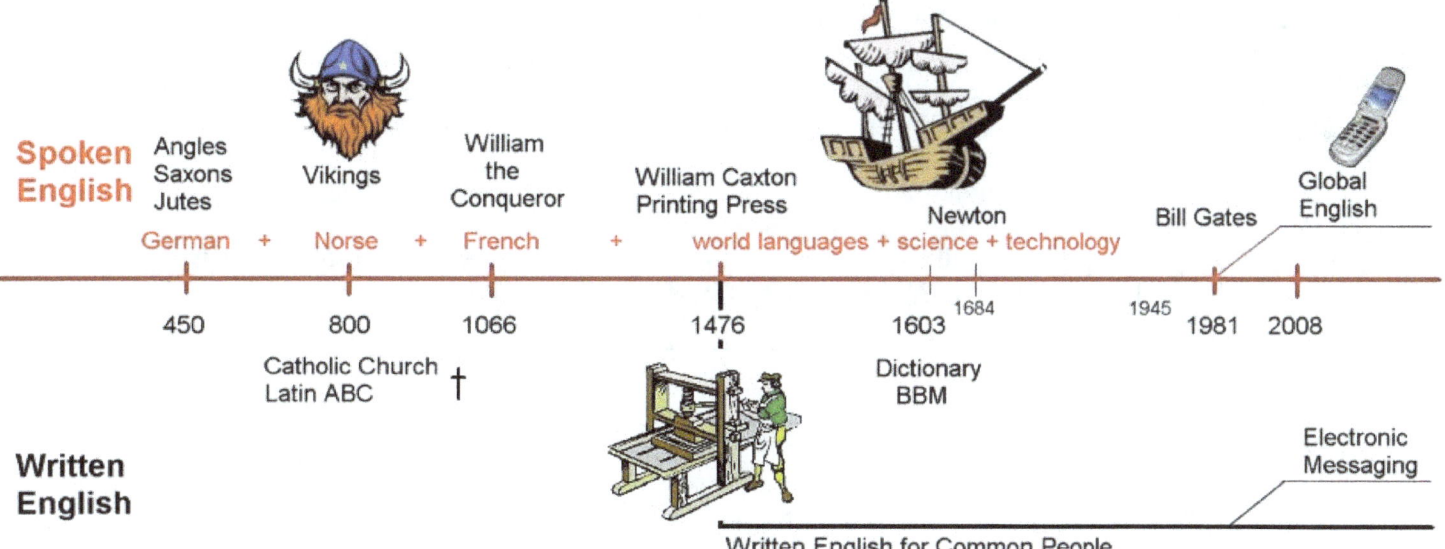

Old English   Middle English   Modern English   Global English

The History of *Spoken* English

450 – German speaking people (Angles, Saxons and Jutes) arrived in Britain, conquered the native (Celtic, Gaelic) people and drove them to the far corners of their island.

750 to **800** – Vikings arrived; more fighting but the winner was not as clear.

- The languages were combined, and then there were two words for many things (e.g. anger/wrath, ill/sick, skin/hide…)
- The German-speaking people on the mainland no longer understood the people in *Angleland*.
- This was the beginning of English and the period called Old English.

1066 – William the Conqueror arrived in England – more fighting. The French won, and thus began several hundred years of French rule in Britain. Then there were three words for many things – German, Norse and French.

> To this day there is no *cow*, *pig* or *sheep* in the grocery store. These were the English peasants' names for the animals they tended in the fields. When the creatures reached the table of the aristocracy in the castle, they were known by French names – boeuf (beef), porc (pork), mouton (mutton)…

The impact of French triggered the 500-year Middle English period.

The History of *Written* English Begins

1476 – William Caxton, an English businessman, bought a printing press from a tradeshow on the continent and set it up in London.

- This gave printed language to common people for the first time.
- Prior to this, English was handwritten by Catholic monks using the Latin alphabet – ABC…
- Caxton didn't know what he was doing, but he did his best. English speaking sounds (40 of them) didn't correspond with the 26 letters of the Latin alphabet, so he made up the spelling as he went along.
- The English spelling and grammar Caxton printed stayed the same for the next 500 years and is known as **Modern English**.

William Caxton didn't just print the language – he carved it in stone.

1603 – They published all Caxton's mistakes in a big book and called it a ***dictionary***. (I like to call it the ***Big Book of Mistakes*** or the BBM.)

> For the next several hundred years, the legendary British fleet dominated the seven seas, claiming land around the world for England. This New World included Hong Kong, India, Australia, etc. Hence the phrase, *The sun never sets on British soil*. Everywhere the mariners sailed, they brought back vocabulary that was added to the burgeoning English language. The trend of adding words to English that began with the Vikings has flourished ever since.

1600 – **William Shakespeare** personally added over **2,000 words** and **phrases** to English that are still in use today (*countless, laughable, to thine ownself be true, pound of flesh, fast and loose, tower of strength, bated breath, love is blind, cold comfort, one fell swoop, it's Greek to me…*)

1667 – **Sir Isaac Newton** published *Principia Mathematica*, the most important book published in the history of science.
- *Principia* was important to language as well as to science.
- Newton introduced words like **gravity, mass, velocity** and paved the way for **English to become the language of science** for centuries to come.

> English has by far the largest vocabulary of any language on earth, and it continues to grow. Last year, the Oxford Dictionary added 2,000 words to its volumes, including words like 24/7, double double, wanna. (Words that have gone out of vogue like haberdashery and confectionary slip out of the Big Book of Mistakes at about the same rate.)

1930 – **David Odgen** published a **Basic English Wordlist** of **850** words.
- This list went to many countries including China, and it formed the basis of the language 1.5 billion people around the world speak today.
- Native English speakers have never heard of it.
- Ogden also published **ten basic grammar rules**.

Ogden's Basic Word List was the beginning of **Global English**.

1945 – The end of **WWII** ushered in the second consecutive English-speaking world power – the USA – to galvanize **English** as the base of global communication.

1981 – **Bill Gates** founded Microsoft. The impact of the **computer** on language and communication is incalculable.

Today

Native English speakers employ hundreds of common grammar structures (with hundreds more exceptions) that remain nameless to most who use them. Grammar is given no more consideration to accuracy than **it just sounds right**. Most native speakers have a *speaking* vocabulary of several hundred thousand words and significantly more **written** words that are understood but not used in normal conversation. Add that number to specific vocabulary for occupations and hobbies, and **one million words** is the estimated number of words in the English language. That number easily doubles when the scientific and biological names of plants and insects are included.

From the timeline, two important things have become clear:

1. *Spoken* English and *Written* English are different languages.

    They have separate histories, symbols, functions and vocabularies.
    The letter/sound relationship is so loose, *writing* and *speaking* are **not directly connected** through the alphabet (as in other languages).

    > For the past 450 years, **English education has been exclusively about *writing***. Although **standard *written* English** has been relatively unaffected over the past 450 years and is still required for scientific and formal communication, *spoken* **English** has evolved at an alarming rate since 1981.

2. **Received Pronunciation (RP) also known as the *Queen's English* is obsolete.** In the world picture of native English-speaking people, the number of people who use the Queen's English or RP is proportionally about the width of a single black line.

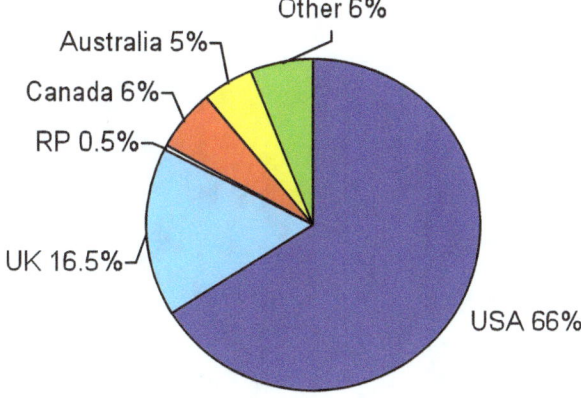

Native English-Speaking Countries

> From the pinnacle of language status in 1476, the *Queen's English* makes up less than one-half of one percent of all native English speakers.
>
> The grammar and pronunciation force-fed to earlier generations is no more.

Appendix 2

Different Ways to Spell the Same Consonant Sound

EPA	Examples	Odd Spellings
/b/	boy, bubble	
/Ch/	chair	cello, nature, cappuccino, truck, watch, Czech
/d/	dog, puddle	water, butter
/f/	fun, waffle	phone, laugh
/g/	girl, egg	example, ghost, guess
/h/	house	who, Juan
/j/	joke	giant, judge, soldier, question
/k/	king	cat, back, school, occur, exit, queen, plaque
/l/	lemon, yellow	
/m/	money, summer	sandwich, Autumn
/n/	no, funny	knee, often, garden, pneumonia
/Ng/	sing	pink, tongue, pumpkin
/p/	paper, happy	hiccough, warm_th
/r/	red, carrot	write, rhyme
/s/	sun, kiss	city, science, psychiatrist, fox, schismatic
/Sh/	shoe	sugar, nation, passion, ocean, machine, schedule
/t/	ten	thyme, shopped, pizza
/Th/	the	
/TH/	thin	
/v/	van	of, Stephen
/w/	we	when, _one, language, queen, choir, po_em
/y/	yes	_unit, _Europe, onion, ewe, hallelujah, b_eautiful
/z/	zoo, puzzle	please, example, scissors
/zh/		beige, television, Asia, azure, echinacea, Taj Mahal

Appendix 3

Silent Consonants

No one knows all the reasons why, but English is plagued with **silent consonants**. They are printed letters that represent no sound and hold no place. Silent consonants can be very confusing for a student whose first language pronounces every letter that is printed – in other words, everyone but native English speakers. To give some idea of the scope of this dilemma, here is a chart with a list of consonants and a few examples of when they are silent.

Consonant	Silent Letters
b	rubber, thumb, plumber, debt, doubt
c	accuse, back, science, arctic
d	wedding, Wednesday, judge, handsome, grandpa
f	raffle
g	nugget, gnat, sign, though, champagne, foreign
h	hour, when, thyme, ghost, rhino, thought, exhaust, hallelujah
k	knee, knight, know, asked
l	balloon, walk, almond, salmon, palm
n	funny, government, hymn, damn, autumn
p	happy, psycho, psalm, pneumonia, pterodactyl, raspberry, receipt
r	carrot, surprise, February
s	dress, island, isle, viscount, Illinois, Arkansas
t	tsunami, listen, whistle, castle, Toronto, wanted, Internet, often, castle, watch, depot
w	write, who, two, answer, sword
x	bateaux, mueslix
y	Hyundai
z	buzz, Szechwan, Czech
ch	yacht, Strachan
th	clothes, asthma, months, lengths, depths

There are many, many more that can be added to this list.

Double consonants only get pronounced once, except for **c** (it can make two sounds right beside itself as in a**cc**ess /**ak**ses/ or su**cc**ess /**suk**ses/).

In North America, double **t** sounds like /d/ in pre**tt**y, bu**tt**er.

English is Crazy

Appendix 4

Different Ways to Spell the Same Vowel Sound

EPA	Color	Examples
/Ay/	**gray**,	g**r**ey m**a**de, **eigh**t, r**ai**n, st**ea**k, th**e**re, s**ue**de, soir**ee**, buff**et**, caf**e**
/a/	**black**	l**au**gh, h**al**f, d**ai**quiri
/Ey/	**green**	m**e**, s**ea**t, sk**i**, mach**i**ne, p**ie**ce, rec**ei**pt, Jud**y**, p**eo**ple, subp**oe**na, arch**ae**ology, q**uay**, **Oi**ja board
/e/	**red**	h**ea**d, s**ai**d, m**a**ny, fr**ie**nd, g**ue**st, j**eo**pardy
/Iy/	**white**	h**eigh**t, **I**, **eye**, m**y**, g**ui**de, b**uy**, b**ye**, p**ie**, **ai**sle, c**o**yote, v**i**olet
/i/	**pink**	pr**e**tty, b**u**sy, b**ee**n, s**ie**ve, m**y**th, b**ui**lt, w**o**men
/Ow/	**gold**	n**o**te, g**o**, kn**ow**, s**ew**, t**oa**st, h**oe**, th**ough**, br**oo**ch, b**eau**, S**eou**l, L**au**sanne, **oh**, f**au**x
/o/	**olive**	f**a**ther, c**ou**gh, c**augh**t, l**aw**ful, br**oa**d, **awe**
/Uw/		c**u**te, n**ew**, y**ou**, tw**o**, d**o**, sh**oe**, j**ui**ce, sch**oo**l, fl**u**, d**eu**ce, b**eau**tiful, l**ieu**, S**iou**x, S**au**lt Ste. Marie
/u/	**mustard**	m**o**ther, w**a**s, d**oe**s, th**e**, c**ou**sin, fl**oo**d, bec**au**se
/^/	**wood**	c**ou**ld, p**u**t, w**o**man
/Oy/	**turquoise**	b**oy**, v**oi**ce, l**aw**yer, Illin**oi**s
/Aw/	**brown**	h**ou**se, pl**ough**

R vowels – **r** is a difficult sound to make and affects the sounds of the vowels around it. In three cases (**Er**, **Ar** and **Or**), the change is so dramatic, three new vowel sounds are created.

/Er/		**pur**ple, h**er**, w**ere**, h**ur**t, f**ir**st, w**or**k, **ear**th, sug**ar**, you'**re**, c**our**tesy, c**o**lonel
/Ar/		**char**coal, h**ear**t, **are**, **R**, s**er**geant, g**uar**d
/Or/		**or**ange, d**oor**, w**ar**, p**our**, m**ore**

Appendix 5

International English Outline for Native Speakers

Language is vocabulary and basic grammar.

- **Intention** is *communication* – Is there understanding or not?

    Shift away from *wrong* grammar or pronunciation

- **Simplified word list** – David Ogden's Basic English 850 words

    One meaning for each word – *I like oranges*, not Oranges are like tangerines.

- **Job specific vocabulary** is added to the basic list as required.

- **Simplified Grammar** – David Ogden lists ten grammar rules.

    No **s** on third person singular – *She go to the bank*.

    Add **s** to non-count nouns – *We have new furnitures.*

- **Pronouns** are vague – agreement is not necessary.

    Mary has a report. *His report is here*.

- **Articles** are loose or non-existent.

    Mary has report. His report here.

- **Pronouns** are elastic - these would roll my grandma over in her grave.

    Him and me went to the store.

    Sing it to Mary and I.

- **Double** word has special power.

    It's cold cold today.

    Oranges and tangerines same same.

- **No assumptions** – be specific.

    The President means nothing.

    The President of the United States is clear.

- **Absolutely no idioms, expressions, or slang**

    Don't *run anything up a flagpole*.
    Nothing is *on thin ice*; there is no *stitch in time*…

Listen with the intention of understanding versus judging.

References[10] – Books

Aiello, L. (2003). *Word P.A.L.S.: A pronunciation and listening skills curriculum for teachers and students of english as a second language.* Mississauga, Ont.: L. Aiello].

Alda, A.,. (2005). *Never have your dog stuffed : And other things I've learned.* New York: Random House.

Avery, P., & Ehrlich, S. (1992). *Teaching american english pronunciation.* Oxford [England]; New York: Oxford University Press.

Baker, A., & Goldstein, S. (1990). *Pronunciation pairs : An introductory course for students of english.* Cambridge [England]; New York: Cambridge University Press.

Beisbier, B. (1994). *Sounds great.* Boston, Mass., U.S.A.: Heinle & Heinle.

Bronstein, A. J. (1960). *The pronunciation of american english; an introduction to phonetics.* New York: Appleton-Century-Crofts.

Bryson, B. (1990). *The mother tongue : English & how it got that way.* New York: W. Morrow.

Christie, A.,. (1963). *The ABC murders.* New York: Pocket Books.

Crystal, D.,. (1995). *The cambridge encyclopedia of the english language.* Cambridge [England]; New York: Cambridge University Press.

Elster, C. H. (1999). *The big book of beastly mispronunciations : The complete opinionated guide for the careful speaker.* Boston: Houghton Mifflin.

Essinger, J.,. (2007). *Spellbound : The surprising origins and astonishing secrets of english spelling.* New York, N.Y.: Bantam Dell.

Graddol, D. (2006). *English next.* London: British Council.

Hancock, M. (1995). *Pronunciation games.* Cambridge; New York: Cambridge University Press.

Lewis, M. (2000). *Teaching collocation : Further developments in the lexical approach.* Hove: Language Teaching Publications.

McLaughlin, B., & National Center for Research on Cultural Diversity and Second Language Learning. (1992). *Myths and misconceptions about second language learning : What every teacher needs to unlearn.* Santa Cruz, CA: National Center for Research on Cultural Diversity and Second Language Learning.

Nilsen, D. L. F., & Nilsen, A. P. (1973). *Pronunciation contrasts in english.* Englewood Cliffs, NJ: Prentice Hall Regents.

Piper, W., & Long, L.,. (2005). *The little engine that could.* New York: Philomel Books : in association with Grosset & Dunlap. Seely, E., & Seely, J.,. (1997). *All about english.* Oxford: Oxford University Press.

Seuss, (1957). *The cat in the hat,.* New York: Random House.

Weinstein, N. J. (1982). *Whaddaya say? : Guided practice in relaxed spoken english.* Englewood Cliffs, N.J.: Prentice-Hall.

Well said : Advanced english pronunciation. Boston: Heinle & Heinle.

---

[10] Retrieved from WorldCat unless otherwise noted.

References – Media

Door-to-door. Carr, W., Macy, W. H., Schachter, S., et al (Directors). (2002).[Video/DVD] Burbank, CA: Warner Home Video.

The miracle worker. Coe, F., Penn, A., Bancroft, A., et al (Directors). (2001).[Video/DVD] Santa Monica, CA: MGM Home Entertainment Inc.

Titanic. DiCaprio, L., Winslet, K., Zane, B., et al (Directors). (1998).[Video/DVD] Hollywood, Calif.: Paramount Home Video.

Dunphy, C. (2007, Jul 30). Teacher's dinners brought together good friends, good food; dedicated ESL instructor known for her love of community. *Toronto Star,* pp. A.17. Retrieved from http://proquest.umi.com/pqdweb?did=1312003591&Fmt=7&clientId=43106&RQT=309&VName=PQD

The wizard of oz. Garland, J., Morgan, F., Bolger, R., et al (Directors). (1999).[Video/DVD] [S.l.]; Burbank, CA: Turner Entertainment Co. ; Warner Home Video.

Bringing down the house. Hoberman, D., Amritraj, A., Filardi, J., et al (Directors). (2003).[Video/DVD] [United States]; Burbank, CA: Touchstone Home Entertainment ; Distributed by Buena Vista Home Entertainment.

Horner, J., Sissel, , Dion, C., Franglen, S., Hinnigan, T., Horner, J., et al. (1997). *Music from the motion picture titanic*. New York, NY: Sony Classical.

Groundhog day. Ramis, H., Murray, B., MacDowell, A., et al (Directors). (1993).[Video/DVD] Burbank, Calif.: Columbia TriStar Home Video.

Gone with the wind. Selznick, D. O., Howard, S. C., Fleming, V., et al (Directors). (1999).[Video/DVD] Burbank, CA: Warner Home Video.

The Simpsons,.Reardon, J, Kirkland, M., et al (Directors). CBS, KPIX, San Francisco.

Erin brockovich. Soderbergh, S., Roberts, J., Finney, A., et al (Directors). (2000).[Video/DVD] Universal City, CA: Universal Studios Home Video.

Twain, S. (2003). *Up!*. Toronto: Mercury Nashville: Distributed in Canada by Universal Music.

Wei, S. (2005). Big dreams pay off for international TV personality. *Today's Canadian, 1*(3), 3.

Welsch, R. (2007, February). From this day forward. *Reader's Digest, 172*

References – Web

Children of the Code. (2009). *Intro article: The history and science of the code and learning to read and comprehend it.* Retrieved 10/03/2009, 2009, from http://www.childrenofthecode.org/cotcintro.htm

Collocation - wikipedia, the free encyclopedia. Retrieved 3/31/2009, 2009, from http://en.wikipedia.org/wiki/Collocation

Delightful homonyms. Retrieved 3/31/2009, 2009, from http://74.125.95.132/search?q=cache:b4p6LDejW54J:www.ierg.net/assets/documents/teach/3pgframes/homonyms.doc+Delightful+Homonyms&cd=1&hl=en&ct=clnk&gl=ca&client=firefox-a

English: Whose language is it? Retrieved 3/31/2009, 2009, from http://secondlanguagewriting.com/explorations/Archives/2007/November/EnglishWhoselanguageisit.html

Feature: RFather: The lord's prayer as a text message. Retrieved 3/27/2009, 2009, from http://www.ship-of-fools.com/features/2001/RFather.html

Finished files - engaging late-breaking articles - wowzio. Retrieved 3/27/2009, 2009, from http://www.wowzio.com/pulse/1176383_finished-files

Free online puzzle maker. Retrieved 3/27/2009, 2009, from http://www.puzzle-maker.com/

FunBrain.com. (2000). *FunBrain.com - the internet's #1 education site for K-8 teachers and kids.*

Guide-to-symbols.com. Retrieved 3/31/2009, 2009, from http://www.guide-to-symbols.com/

International listening association. Retrieved 3/31/2009, 2009, from http://www.listen.org/Templates/factoids.htm

The meanings and origins of sayings and phrases | list of sayings | english sayings | idiom definitions | idiom examples | idiom origins | list of idioms | idiom dictionary | meaning of idioms. Retrieved 3/31/2009, 2009, from http://www.phrases.org.uk/

Ogden's basic english. Retrieved 3/27/2009, 2009, from http://ogden.basic-english.org/

Optical illusions. Retrieved 3/27/2009, 2009, from http://www.optillusions.com/

Punctuation definition | dictionary.com. Retrieved 3/31/2009, 2009, from http://dictionary.reference.com/browse/punctuation

The quote garden - quotes, sayings, quotations, verses. Retrieved 3/27/2009, 2009, from http://www.quotegarden.com/

Wu, C. *Cultural gestures.* Retrieved 26/02/2009, 2009, from http://soc302.tripod.com/soc_302rocks/id6.html

Yankee. the american heritage® dictionary of the english language: Fourth edition. 2000. Retrieved 3/27/2009, 2009, from http://www.bartleby.com/61/60/Y0006000.html

English is Crazy

Notes

Notes

English is Crazy

Notes

Notes

Thompson Language Center
PRODUCT LIST

English is Crazy — the definitive speaking guide

An innovative working textbook for the fastest method for learning to speak English ever developed. Speaking isn't writing said out loud.

The English Phonetic Alphabet Workbook — over 200 pronunciation activities

Companion to Chapter One of **English is Crazy** – these exercises to instil the 40 sounds of the English language, suitable for Basic to Advanced learners.

Speaking Made Simple — Course Curriculum

A stand-alone, step by step, 360 page speaking course based on the patterns of spoken English introduced in **English is Crazy**. Treasured by a wide range of ESL/EFL institutions worldwide since 2011.

How Do You Say? — Spelling, Pronunciation and Expressions Dictionary

The 2,000 most common words in English organized by main vowel sound from the *Thompson Vowel Chart* featured in **English is Crazy**. Easy access to how words are spelled, what they mean, how they are pronounced, and how they are used in expressions. Learners LOVE it.

Backpacker's Guide to Teaching English
— for casual instructors with no **previous training** or **experience**

BOOK 1 **Cracking the Code** – on Pronunciation
BOOK 2 **Need For Speed** – on Conversation
BOOK 3 **You Don't Say** – on Fluency

ABC Facilitated Reading - An interactive literacy system for learning to read at home

This revolutionary program effectively addresses crazy English spelling in a simple, interactive process parents and leaners enjoy. **Facilitated learning** in general evokes security, creativity, confidence, inclusion, relationship, life-skills, and fun.

A range of educational Poster and Flashcard PDFs are available from
www.thompsonlanguagecenter.com

For more information or to order products, contact judy@thompsonlanguagecenter.com

Changing the way the world learns

© Judy Thompson 2009

English is Crazy
"Inglish iz krAyzEy."

www.ingramcontent.com/pod-product-compliance
Lightning Source LLC
Chambersburg PA
CBHW081350230426
43667CB00017B/2780